Still GOLD'n

CELEBRATING SPOKANE ONE MEAL AT A TIME

THE JUNIOR LEAGUE OF SPOKANE

The Junior League of Spokane is an organization of women committed to promoting voluntarism and
to improving the community through the effective action and leadership of trained volunteers.
Its purpose is exclusively educational and charitable.

The Junior League of Spokane reaches out to women of all races, religions, and national origins
who demonstrate an interest in and commitment to voluntarism.

CELEBRATING SPOKANE ONE MEAL AT A TIME

Published by The Junior League of Spokane
Copyright © 2007
The Junior League of Spokane
1315 North Napa Street
Spokane, Washington 99202
509-328-2801
First Printing: 2007 10,000 copies
Library of Congress Number: 2006922680
ISBN: 0-9646784-1-1

Cover photography and photos on pages 29, 47, 102, 114 © Barros & Barros
Lithograph "Childhood Express" Riverfront Park, Spokane, Washington © 1993 Ken Spiering,
Red Wagon photo pages 6, 21 © 1993 Ken Spiering, photographed by Berit McAllister
Black Rock Golf Course photo page 11 courtesy of The Club at Black Rock © Rob Perry
Back cover photography and all photos on pages 9, 13, 15, 17, 39, 61, 87, 109, and 127 © courtesy of *The Spokesman-Review*

Edited, Designed, and Manufactured by
Favorite Recipes® Press
An imprint of

FRP

P.O. Box 305142
Nashville, Tennessee 37230
800-358-0560

Art Director and Book Design: Steve Newman
Project Editor: Anna Watson

Printed in China

TABLE OF

Contents

A History of Helping

The Junior League of Spokane

As early as 1932, the Junior League of Spokane was striving to help the community. "Sixty-one of 100 layettes (baby clothes) completed for the Red Cross" reads one entry in the secretary's minutes for that year. The world watched warily as Adolf Hiltler became Chancellor of Germany in 1933, and soon the Red Cross and the Junior League with them would be sorely needed internationally as well as locally.

Indeed, throughout the 1930s, the Junior League would continue to partner with the Red Cross, making Christmas bags for those in need, bags for soldiers, and cash donations. By 1940, the bandage unit of the Red Cross had become the "Junior League Red Cross Unit."

Children and families were the League's primary focus even during those turbulent times. Junior League minutes from 1932 (the earliest year available) reflect that a children's welfare clinic was in operation. By 1937, a prenatal clinic was serving up to thirty-five families per morning.

When the United States finally formally entered World War II on December 7, 1941, after the attack on Pearl Harbor, the Junior League was there to heed the call. The League furnished and decorated the Air Force's officers' quarters at Geiger Field, purchased defense savings bonds, and started a service at Ft. George Wright to "furnish comfort and games" to Air Force personnel who were convalescing there.

During 1942, as the conflict intensified, new Junior League members (called provisionals) were required to take a Red Cross course on being a nurse's aide before admission to the League. The following year was the biggest year ever at the Junior League's Child Health Association, with 1,801 children recorded as patients!

By 1945, in addition to all its other projects, the Junior League helped start the blood bank in Spokane. Two League members at a time assisted the doctors and nurses three days a week. In addition, every League member was required to help at the Child Health Clinic as well as the Prenatal Clinic. Quilts were made for the Red Cross and dances were organized for soldiers on leave. Times were very busy!

When the war ended in September 1945, the country and the world breathed a collective sigh of relief. Now the Junior League could focus on other issues that needed attention. During the 1940s, there was no vaccine for polio as there is today. Every summer, thousands of adults and children became gravely ill or died. Permanent paralysis (as suffered by President Franklin D. Roosevelt) was not uncommon. In 1946, the Junior League joined the National Foundation for Infantile Paralysis in a polio preparedness effort.

By 1950, the Junior League had expanded to fill even more community needs as the nation entered the Korean War. The League sponsored a recreation center together with the Parks Department near Glover Field. The center featured such activities as dancing classes for kindergartners through fourth graders and was open two nights a week for teenagers. Such activities as the Red Cross Drive, the Cancer Drive, and the Polio Drive kept members busy.

In March of 1951, Mr. Joel Ferris wrote a thank-you to the Junior League on behalf of the Eastern Washington State Historical Society and Museum (the precursor to our modern-day Museum of Northwest Arts and Culture) for all the work the Junior League had exhibited in preparing and volunteering as docents.

As in the early days, the Junior League was also active in the current events of the day. In 1958, as the Cold War unfolded, the League hosted talks by the United States Air Force and the Strategic Air Command on civil defense. The League established a speech clinic for the prevention of speech disorders in preschool children and a clinic for emotionally disturbed children, placing them at the forefront of issues in mental health.

As the 1960s embroiled the country with political unrest and widespread social change, once again the Junior League proved equal to the task. In 1965, the Junior League was nominated for a Lane Bryant award for the work done in the field of mental health. Indeed, the Spokane Junior League established a community mental health clinic that continues its work today. League members also received an award from Morningstar Boys' Ranch for the number of service hours provided there by members.

By 1970, the mental health center was still going strong. Support of the arts continued, as the Junior League hosted an Art School and supported KSPS (public television). Once again, the Junior League recognized societal changes such as more women working outside the home. This trend created different needs in the community that the League addressed. In 1971, the League was involved in a program for children and working parents called Community Coordinated Childcare.

A sad new trend in society that surfaced in the early 1970s was the recognition of child abuse as a pervasive problem. The League responded with a program called SCAN (Suspected Child Abuse and Neglect Center), which is still in existence today. Over the course of three years, the League would spend approximately $32,000 to get the center up and running to meet this vital community need for children. From the work done in SCAN, members also saw a need for a crisis nursery to provide respite care for parents during difficult times when they may be at risk for abusing their child. From this came the Vanessa Behan Crisis Nursery, which continues to provide this important service.

The 1980s found the Junior League still involved in many things established earlier, such as SCAN, and many new projects as well. Working with the handicapped and trying to increase community awareness was the focus of the League's physical rehabilitation advocacy effort. The Funding Information Center was also started at this time, providing in-depth information on funding by corporations and private foundations for nonprofit organizations and individuals.

Cultural education continued to be a strong area of interest to the League. The Junior League was one of three organizations to get Public Radio "on air" in Spokane, with a donation of $20,000, and was also involved in such projects as the Riverfront Festival Board and the Spokane Arts Commission. Career development classes were sponsored by the League for kids and adults interested in working. Over nine hundred children received the training in Spokane schools in 1980 alone.

By the mid-1980s, the public was becoming aware of issues such as homelessness and increasing diversity. In 1986, the Junior League started the Crosswalk program with Volunteers of America in hopes of helping runaways living on the streets. The program is needed more than ever and is still going strong. Increasing diversity was the focus of the Diversification Task Force created within the League, to recruit women of color for League membership, one of the first organizations in Spokane to do so.

As the 1980s continued, ensuring a rich environment for kids continued to be a strong focus, and in 1990, the League came through with the Centennial Children's Art Project. The project entailed creating an enormous sculpture of a Radio Flyer red wagon that is also a slide for children. The sculpture was an immediate success when placed in its permanent location in Riverfront Park, and it continues to delight young and old alike to this day.

Some other ways the League continued its commitment to the young that arose during the 1990s, were Project Lead and Kids on the Block. Project Lead was a program aimed at teaching teenagers to volunteer in the community. Kids on the Block was a puppet program designed for younger children fourth grade through sixth grade to help them understand those with special needs. The Kaleidoscope program started by the Junior League at this time provided arts activities for hundreds of kids.

The League also continued to expand its involvement with children affected by abuse and neglect. A new program to provide respite care to foster parents, the STAR Foster Parent program, began. League members started the My Bag project for kids newly removed from their homes due to abuse or neglect. Children in this situation often have literally nothing but the clothes on their backs. The My Bag project gave each child a bag of such things as a toothbrush, a blanket, books, and a teddy bear to help provide some comfort to these traumatized kids. My Bag is also still going strong.

With the passage into the new millennium, the Junior League is still finding ways to contribute to the Spokane community. Current projects include Rebuilding Together, a national program that the Junior League partners with every year. The program provides badly needed "rebuilding" of homes in need of repair where the residents are unable to do it. Recipients often are elderly, or single parents with small children. Volunteers from the Junior League and other organizations meet for a day of painting (inside and out), gardening, even plumbing and rewiring for homes in need of help.

Foster Santa Breakfast is a program currently held every year by the Junior League for foster parents and children in Spokane. Every year on a weekend in early December, foster kids and their foster parents gather for a festive holiday breakfast. Children get to visit with Santa, who arrives on a fire truck, and pick out a gift for themselves and either their foster or biological parent. Numerous Christmas trees with gift themes, as well as bikes and other gifts, are raffled off. Every family gets a turkey to take home. It is a day of cheer for people who badly need it.

Impact Spokane is a series of "done in a day" projects the Junior League sponsors or helps with throughout Spokane. Examples of such projects include refurbishing the recreation room at Anna Ogden Hall, helping with the Halloween Carnival at St. Luke's Rehabilitation Hospital, and working for the Guild School penny drive. These projects allow members to make an impact all over the community.

Looking to the future, the Junior League's next area of focus is mentoring young women in the community. Reaching out to young people is just as critical as ever in these uncertain times. We in the Junior League hope to continue the important and proud work done by our members for the last eighty-one years here. Your purchase of this cookbook will help us to do this. Thank you, and we hope you and your loved ones enjoy it!

Chapter Sponsors

THE SPOKESMAN-REVIEW

Great Harvest Bread Co.

STERLING SAVINGS BANK

Page Sponsors

Washington Trust Bank

THE DAVENPORT HOTEL

EZ LOADER

AESTHETIC IMAGE
PREMIER MEDICAL SPA

Northwest
FARM CREDIT SERVICES

BLACK ROCK

Supporters

SLACK & COMBS
ORTHODONTICS

DCI·ENGINEERS
D'AMATO CONVERSANO INC.

Spring

Lilac Spring Brunch

Garlic Pepper Cheese Rounds
page 31

Sausage Phyllo Breakfast Strudel
page 44

Incredibly Good Blueberry Muffins
page 56

Greenbluff Strawberry Spinach Salad
page 76

Frozen Lemon Soufflé
page 144

Spring Picnic in the Park

Marvelous Muffuletta
page 93

Greek Vegetable Salad
page 78

Angelic Almond Bars
page 147

Page Sponsor: *Washington Trust Bank*

Springtime in Riverfront Park. Seagulls fly above the colorful flowers and Spokane's signature clock tower.
Photograph courtesy of The Spokesman-Review.

Summer

Lake Barbecue

Deviled Shrimp with Spicy Cocktail Sauce
page 28

Honey Lime Chicken
page 103

Spicy Corn on the Cob
page 80

Spokane Blue Spinach Salad
page 75

Huckleberry Crumble
page 132

"Fall Off the Dock" Lemonade
page 35

Hoopfest Happening

Roasted Pepper and Artichoke Tapenade
page 29

Grilled Prime Rib of Beef with Garlic and Rosemary
page 88

Mediterranean Pasta Salad
page 74

Margarita Cheesecake
page 134

Page Sponsor: *The Club at Black Rock*

The gently sloping hills of the Black Rock golf course overlook Lake Coeur d'Alene.
Photograph courtesy of The Club at Black Rock.

Back-to-School Celebration

To "Brie or Not To Brie"
page 31

Straight Out of the Garden Red Sauce
page 115

Northwest Spinach Salad with Apple and Cheddar
page 75

Aunt Betty's Dinner Rolls
page 58

Apricot Logs
page 148

Fall Color Fun

Cougar Gold, Apple and Onion Soup
page 64

Bourbon Pecan Chicken
page 107

Mashed Potatoes and Parsnips
page 83

Autumn in Spokane Salad
page 72

Washington Apple Cake
page 136

Page Sponsor: *Northwest Farm Credit Services*

Amber Waves of Grain. A combine works a wheat field south of Rosalia, as the area glows orange from the setting sun.
Photograph courtesy of The Spokesman-Review.

Home in Front of the Fire

Ring in the New Year

Page Sponsor: *Aesthetic Image*

A swan elegantly lifts its wings on a cruise through the icy waters of Manito Pond.
Photograph courtesy of The Spokesman-Review.

The ABCs—Great Ways to Start

APPETIZERS, BEVERAGES & COCKTAILS

Chapter Sponsor: *The Spokesman-Review*

The smoked salmon appetizer at Milford's Fish House is one of their top sellers.
They smoke the fish right at the restaurant. Photograph courtesy of The Spokesman-Review.

Chicken Satay with Peanut Sauce

2 tablespoons sugar
1 tablespoon curry powder
3 tablespoons soy sauce
1 teaspoon minced garlic
1/2 teaspoon salt
1/2 teaspoon pepper
2 tablespoons vegetable oil
3 tablespoons lemon juice
2 tablespoons hot chili paste
6 boneless skinless chicken
   breasts, pounded to
   1/4-inch thickness
   Peanut Sauce

Combine the sugar, curry powder, soy sauce, garlic, salt, pepper, oil, lemon juice and chili paste in a large bowl and mix well. Cut the chicken into long thin strips and add to the marinade. Marinate, covered, in the refrigerator overnight.

Preheat the grill. Remove the chicken strips from the marinade and thread onto skewers, discarding the marinade. Grill for 5 to 7 minutes or until the chicken is cooked through. Serve with Peanut Sauce.

Serves 12

Peanut Sauce

1/2 cup finely chopped onion
1 teaspoon minced garlic
1 tablespoon sesame oil
1 cup creamy peanut butter
1 teaspoon curry powder
1/4 cup packed dark brown sugar
1/2 teaspoon salt
2 teaspoons hot chili paste
1 1/2 tablespoons lemon juice
1 (14-ounce) can light
   coconut milk
1 to 2 tablespoons hot water

Sauté the onion and garlic in the sesame oil in a small saucepan over medium heat until the onion is tender. Add the peanut butter, curry powder, brown sugar, salt and chili paste and mix well. Add the lemon juice and mix well. Add the coconut milk and hot water, stirring constantly. Cook over low heat until heated through, stirring occasionally. Serve with Chicken Satay or over rice.

Makes about 3 cups

Grilled Pork Tenderloin with Plum Sauce

1 (1¹/2-pound) pork tenderloin
¹/3 cup honey
1 cup soy sauce
  Freshly ground pepper to taste
  Hot mustard
  Toasted sesame seeds
  Plum Sauce

Place the tenderloin in a shallow nonaluminum container. Combine the honey and soy sauce in a small bowl and mix well. Season the tenderloin with pepper and coat evenly with the honey-soy mixture. Marinate, covered, in the refrigerator for 2 hours, turning the meat occasionally.

Preheat the grill. Remove the tenderloin from the marinade, reserving the marinade for basting. Grill over medium-hot coals until browned on all sides. Cover and grill for 20 to 30 minutes longer or until an instant-read thermometer inserted into the center registers 150 to 155 degrees, turning occasionally and brushing with the reserved marinade. Discard any remaining marinade.

Chill, covered, in the refrigerator overnight or until completely cool.

Remove to a cutting board and cut into ¹/4-inch slices. Arrange on a platter and serve with hot mustard, toasted sesame seeds and Plum Sauce.

Serves 4 to 6

Plum Sauce

1¹/2 teaspoons dry mustard
1¹/2 teaspoons cider vinegar
 ¹/8 teaspoon salt
  Small pinch of dried red
  pepper flakes
  Small sliver of garlic
 ¹/2 cup plum jam or apricot jam
 ¹/2 teaspoon soy sauce
 1 teaspoon grated fresh gingerroot

Combine the mustard, vinegar, salt, red pepper flakes, garlic, jam, soy sauce and gingerroot in a small saucepan and mix well. Cook over medium heat until the mixture bubbles, stirring occasionally. Remove from the heat and let cool completely before serving.

Makes ¹/2 cup

"Ancient Chinese Secret" Pork

1/2 teaspoon salt
1/4 teaspoon pepper
1/4 teaspoon Chinese
   five-spice powder
  1 teaspoon cooking sherry
  2 tablespoons soy sauce
  3 tablespoons hoisin sauce
1/2 teaspoon red food coloring
  1 (1 1/2-pound) pork tenderloin
   Honey (optional)
   Chinese hot mustard
   Sesame seeds

Combine the salt, pepper, five-spice powder, sherry, soy sauce, hoisin sauce and food coloring in a small bowl and mix well.

Place the tenderloin in a nonaluminum container and cover with the marinade, turning to coat evenly. Marinate, covered, in the refrigerator overnight, turning occasionally.

Preheat the oven to 350 degrees. Cover the bottom of a 9×13-inch baking pan with foil and place a roasting rack in the pan. Remove the tenderloin from the marinade to the rack, discarding the marinade.

Bake for 25 minutes and turn. Bake for 25 minutes longer or until an instant-read thermometer inserted into the thickest portion of the tenderloin registers 150 to 155 degrees. Brush the tenderloin with honey during baking if desired. Chill, covered, overnight or until completely cool.

Slice thinly and serve with Chinese hot mustard and sesame seeds for dipping.

Serves 4 to 6

Hoisin is a sweet sauce with garlic often found in the Asian section of a well-stocked supermarket. Chinese five-spice powder is a unique blend of ground cinnamon, fennel, star anise, cloves, and Szechwan pepper that is found in all types of Asian cuisine. Dishes with Asian flair are found throughout the Pacific Northwest due to its proximity to the Pacific Rim.

Pancetta Prawns

8 ounces thinly sliced pancetta
1 pound fresh prawns, peeled
and deveined
Olive oil
Old Bay seasoning

Preheat the oven to 400 degrees. Cut each slice of pancetta into thirds. Wrap each prawn with a thin strip of pancetta and place on a baking sheet lined with baking parchment.

Drizzle the prawns with olive oil and sprinkle with Old Bay seasoning. Bake for 10 minutes or until the prawns are pink and the pancetta is just beginning to crisp. Do not overbake or the prawns will become tough.

Serves 4 to 6

A Walk in the Park—Part I

A visit to Spokane simply would not be complete without a visit to Riverfront Park, located in the heart of the city along the river. Many amenities were constructed in the park when Spokane hosted the 1974 World's Fair, including an IMAX theater and a gondola. Visitors can ride the newly renovated aerial gondola for a breathtaking view of the Spokane Falls. The park is also home to the famous Looff Carousel, a national historic landmark created in 1909 by Charles Looff. The carousel consists of wonderful horses and other animals, painstakingly carved by hand. Generations of children have reached for its brass ring. In case this is not enough, there is another attraction especially dear to the Spokane Junior League's heart (because we sponsored it): the Red Wagon sculpture. Created in 1989 for the Centennial Celebration of Children by artist Ken Spiering, it is a twelve-foot-high Radio Flyer Red Wagon with a "handle" that is a children's slide. It is always fun to watch the children laughing as they enjoy a quick ride down.

Asian Crab Cakes

8 ounces fresh lump crab meat, drained and flaked
1/4 cup mayonnaise
1 tablespoon Asian chili sauce
1 teaspoon fresh lemon juice
1 teaspoon sesame oil
1 egg, beaten
1/2 teaspoon salt
1 cup panko
1/4 cup canola oil
2 tablespoons sesame seeds

Combine the crab meat, mayonnaise, chili sauce, lemon juice, sesame oil, egg and salt in a bowl and mix well. Add 1/4 cup of the panko to the mixture and stir gently to combine. Chill, covered, in the refrigerator for 1 hour.

Shape the mixture into patties 1 1/2 inches in diameter. Place the remaining 3/4 cup panko in a bowl. Dip each patty into the panko, turning to coat evenly.

Fry the patties in the canola oil in a heavy cast-iron skillet for 1 minute per side or until golden brown. Drain on paper towels and sprinkle with the sesame seeds.

Makes 12 miniature crab cakes

Marinated Asparagus

Asparagus
1 pound asparagus, trimmed
2 tablespoons water

Shallot Marinade
2 tablespoons finely chopped shallots
1 teaspoon salt
1/2 teaspoon pepper
1 teaspoon sugar
2 tablespoons spicy Dijon mustard
2 tablespoons raspberry wine vinegar
6 tablespoons olive oil
Raspberries or edible fresh flowers

For the asparagus, place the asparagus and water in a large sealable plastic bag and seal partially, leaving some room for steam to escape. Microwave on Medium for 3 to 4 minutes or until the asparagus spears are bright green and tender-crisp; drain.

For the marinade, blend the shallots, salt, pepper, sugar and mustard in a small bowl. Add the vinegar and mix well. Add the olive oil slowly in a steady stream, whisking constantly until the marinade is thick and creamy.

Pour the marinade into the bag with the asparagus; seal the bag. Marinate in the refrigerator for 4 hours to overnight. Remove from the bag and place on a platter.

To serve, garnish with raspberries or edible fresh flowers.

Serves 6 to 8

Spicy Dilled Green Beans

1 teaspoon cayenne pepper
8 garlic cloves
4 sprigs of dill weed
2 pounds green beans, trimmed
2¹/₂ cups white vinegar
2¹/₂ cups water
¹/₄ teaspoon salt

Place ¹/₄ teaspoon of the cayenne pepper, 2 garlic cloves and 1 sprig of dill weed into each of four clean wide-mouth 1-pint canning jars. Pack the beans vertically into the jars. Bring the vinegar, water and salt to a boil in a saucepan over high heat. Pour the liquid over the beans to within ¹/₂ inch of the jar top and seal with two-piece lids. Process in a boiling water bath for 7 minutes, starting the time when the water returns to a boil. Remove from the water and cool. Let "season" for 30 days for best flavor.

Makes 4 jars green beans, with 4 servings per jar

Crab-Stuffed Cremini Mushrooms

¹/₄ cup finely minced carrots
¹/₄ cup finely minced celery
1 tablespoon finely minced shallots
3 tablespoons salted butter
¹/₂ cup heavy cream
1 cup fresh Dungeness crab meat, drained and flaked
¹/₄ teaspoon white pepper
1 tablespoon minced fresh tarragon (optional)
24 large cremini mushroom caps, stems removed
2 tablespoons sea salt
2 tablespoons grated Parmesan or asiago cheese
¹/₂ lemon

Sauté the carrots, celery and shallots in the butter in a saucepan over medium heat until tender. Add the cream and bring to a boil. Let the mixture boil until reduced by half, stirring occasionally. Remove from the heat and let cool. Add the crab meat, stirring gently to combine. Season with white pepper and tarragon; chill in the refrigerator.

Preheat the oven to 375 degrees. Place the mushroom caps on a baking sheet and season the interior of each with a pinch of the salt. Place 1 tablespoon of the crab mixture in each mushroom cap. Sprinkle with the cheese. Bake for 13 to 15 minutes or until the mushrooms are heated through. Remove to a platter and squeeze the lemon over the mushrooms.

Variation: Bake the mushrooms on a cedar plank, available in most gourmet cooking stores. It will add a nice flavor and will fill the house with a wonderful cedar aroma.

Makes 24 mushrooms

Magnificent Stuffed Mushrooms with Bacon, Feta and Spinach

8 ounces bacon, sliced
1 cup chopped onion
1 (10-ounce) package frozen spinach, thawed, drained and squeezed dry
4 ounces feta cheese, crumbled (about 3/4 cup)
4 ounces cream cheese, softened
1/4 teaspoon dried crushed red pepper
  Salt and black pepper to taste
2 3/4 pounds button mushrooms, stemmed (about 48)

Fry the bacon in a large heavy skillet over medium heat for 8 minutes or until crisp. Drain on paper towels, reserving 2 teaspoons of the bacon drippings. Coarsely crumble the bacon.

Sauté the onion in the reserved bacon drippings in a large heavy skillet over medium heat for 5 minutes or until the onion is tender. Remove the onion to a bowl and let cool. Add the bacon, spinach, feta cheese, cream cheese and crushed red pepper. Season with salt and black pepper to taste.

Spoon 1 heaping teaspoon of the filling into each mushroom cap. (Filled mushrooms can be prepared 1 day ahead. Chill, covered, in the refrigerator.)

Preheat the oven to 375 degrees. Bake the mushrooms for 10 minutes or until heated through. Remove to a platter and serve warm.

Makes 48 mushrooms

Rich and decadent, these are a surefire way to please a crowd. Use mushrooms that are slightly larger than bite-size because they will shrink a little when cooked.

Phyllo Mushroom Delights

4   cups coarsely chopped
    mushrooms (portobello, shiitake,
    white or brown)
3   garlic cloves, minced
2   tablespoons butter
1   cup (4 ounces) shredded
    Gruyère cheese
1   tablespoon chopped fresh sage
1   tablespoon chopped
    fresh marjoram
1/4 teaspoon salt
1/4 teaspoon coarse pepper
1   (16-ounce) package frozen phyllo
    dough, thawed
1/2 cup (1 stick) butter, melted

Sauté the mushrooms and garlic in 2 tablespoons butter in a large heavy skillet over medium heat for 10 minutes. Remove from the heat and let cool slightly. Stir in the cheese, sage, marjoram, salt and pepper. Preheat the oven to 400 degrees. Unroll the phyllo dough. Place one sheet on a flat work surface and cover the remaining with a damp cloth or paper towel. Brush the sheet of phyllo lightly with butter. Spread 1 tablespoon of the mushroom mixture in a thin line along one edge of the sheet and roll up tightly to enclose the filling. Twist the ends and place on a baking parchment-lined baking sheet. Repeat the procedure with the remaining phyllo sheets and mushroom mixture. Bake for 10 minutes or until golden brown.

Makes 15 servings

A Walk in the Park—Part II

In Spokane, we take our parks seriously. There are acres and acres of them, encompassing everything from conservation land to neighborhood parks designed for fun and relaxation. A fine example is Manito Park, located on Spokane's South Hill. Manito Park spans ninety acres with a breathtaking variety of spots to enjoy nature. The lower part of Manito Park has a large pond with a fountain where ducks, swans, and turtles bask in the summer sunshine.

During the summer, Manito Park is the perfect place for a stroll that delights the eye and refreshes the spirit. For children and families, there are play structures and slides to explore and long winding paths under the canopy of the trees. It truly is a magical place.

Milford's Smoked Salmon Appetizer

1 (7-ounce) piece of smoked
  salmon (see Note)
4 to 5 slices focaccia bread
3 ounces cream cheese, softened
1 hard-cooked egg
1 to 2 teaspoons finely chopped
  red onion
1 to 2 teaspoons capers, rinsed

Arrange the fish and the bread slices on one side of a serving plate. Place the cream cheese on the opposite side of the plate.

Separate the white of the egg from the yolk. Grate the white and yolk separately. Arrange the grated white and yolk, the onion and capers in separate rows like a rainbow across the center of the plate.

Note: To smoke your own salmon, combine 2 cups packed brown sugar, 1 cup kosher salt and 1 gallon water in a large nonreactive container and mix well. Place two to three whole salmon (cleaned, with skin on to preserve the moisture) in the brine and let soak for 12 to 24 hours. Remove the salmon, discarding the brine. Rinse the fish thoroughly and pat dry. Sprinkle the salmon with freshly ground pepper and place on the rack of a smoker. Smoke the salmon using the manufacturer's instructions; smoking time will vary depending on the size of the fish.

Serves 2 to 4

Shrimp Ceviche

Citrus Marinade

    Juice of 3 lemons
    Juice of 3 limes
1/4 teaspoon El Mexicano Pico
    de Gallo seasoning
1/4 teaspoon seasoned salt
1/4 teaspoon cumin
    Salt and pepper to taste

Ceviche

2 cucumbers, diced
3 tomatoes, diced
1/2 sweet white onion, minced
2 garlic cloves, minced
2 jalapeño chiles, minced
2 carrots, diced
1/2 to 1 pound peeled baby shrimp
1/2 to 1 package imitation crab flakes
    Chopped cilantro to taste
1 avocado, diced

For the marinade, combine the lemon juice, lime juice, pico de gallo seasoning, seasoned salt, cumin, salt and pepper in a bowl and mix well.

For the ceviche, combine the cucumbers, tomatoes, onion, garlic, jalapeño chiles, carrots, shrimp, crab flakes and cilantro and mix well. Add the avocado and the marinade and stir gently to combine.

Chill, covered, in the refrigerator for 6 to 8 hours before serving. Serve with pita chips or tortilla chips.

Serves 6 to 8

Deviled Shrimp

Marinade

- 1/4 cup olive oil
- 1/2 cup fresh lemon juice
- 1 tablespoon red wine vinegar
- 2 garlic cloves, crushed
- 1 tablespoon dry mustard
- 1 tablespoon salt
- 1 bay leaf, crumbled

Shrimp

- 2 pounds large peeled cooked shrimp
- 1 lemon, thinly sliced
- 1 red onion, thinly sliced
- 1 cup pitted black olives
  Chopped parsley to taste
  Spicy Cocktail Sauce

For the marinade, whisk the olive oil, lemon juice, vinegar, garlic, mustard, salt and bay leaf in a bowl until blended.

For the shrimp, place the shrimp, lemon, onion, olives and parsley in a large sealable plastic bag. Pour the marinade over the shrimp mixture and seal the bag. Chill in the refrigerator for 1 to 3 hours. Drain the shrimp, discarding the marinade. Serve with Spicy Cocktail Sauce.

Serves 6 to 8

Spicy Cocktail Sauce

- 1 teaspoon creamy horseradish
- 1 teaspoon water
- 3/4 cup ketchup
- 1 tablespoon white wine vinegar
- 1 teaspoon Worcestershire sauce

Combine the horseradish, water, ketchup, vinegar and Worcestershire sauce in a bowl and mix well. Chill, covered, until ready to serve.

Serves 6 to 8

Roasted Pepper and Artichoke Tapenade

1 (7-ounce) jar roasted red bell
   peppers, drained and chopped
1 (6-ounce) jar marinated artichoke
   hearts, drained and chopped
1/4 cup minced fresh parsley
1/2 cup (2 ounces) grated
   Parmesan cheese
1/3 cup olive oil
1/4 cup capers, drained
4 garlic cloves, chopped
1 tablespoon lemon juice
   Salt and pepper to taste

Combine the bell peppers, artichoke hearts, parsley, cheese, olive oil, capers, garlic and lemon juice in a bowl and mix well. Season with salt and pepper to taste. Serve with pita chips or crackers.

Serves 4 to 6

A Walk in the Park—Part III

Spokane has the famous Duncan Gardens, a formal garden planted exclusively with annual flowering plants every summer, and the Rose Hill, with every imaginable rose variety. The perennial garden delights the eye with hostas, lavender, coreopsis, iris, and more. The Japanese Garden is the picture of serenity with graceful lace leaf maples silhouetted around a quiet pond with colorful koi. Lilacs abound on the Lilac Hill. What else would you expect from the Lilac City?

The beauty of Manito Park is just the beginning. Spokanites and visitors can also enjoy Finch Arboretum, home to great towering trees that provide huge piles of leaves perfect for jumping into, as well as a blaze of fall color that is truly dazzling. There are countless neighborhood parks throughout the city, giving folks a much-needed place to enjoy the outdoors and the four seasons in all their glory.

Bacon Avocado Salsa

3 avocados, chopped and
  pits reserved
4 to 5 strips bacon, crisp-cooked
  and crumbled
1 large tomato, chopped
3 green onions, chopped
1 teaspoon garlic powder
1/2 cup green hot sauce
  Crumbled crisp-cooked bacon
  Chopped green onions

Combine the avocados, bacon, tomato, green onions, garlic powder and hot sauce in a bowl and mix gently, taking care not to smash the avocados. Chill, covered, in the refrigerator until ready to serve. Garnish with crumbled bacon and green onions.

Note: To keep the avocados fresh, place the avocado pits in the salsa until ready to serve. To serve, remove and discard the pits.

Serves 4 to 6

Fruit Salsa

2 mangoes, finely chopped
1 avocado, cubed
1 red bell pepper, seeded
  and minced
1/4 cup cilantro, chopped
2 green onions, minced
2 tablespoons fresh
  gingerroot, minced
2 tablespoons orange juice
2 tablespoon brown sugar
2 teaspoons Asian chile sauce

Combine the mangoes, avocado, bell pepper, cilantro, green onions, gingerroot, orange juice, brown sugar and chile sauce in a bowl and mix well. Serve with pulled pork or grilled fish.

Note: Asian chile sauce is a blend of hot chile pepper, garlic, oil and salt. It can be found in well-stocked grocery stores.

Serves 4 to 6

To "Brie or Not to Brie"

1 (15-ounce) wheel Brie cheese
2 tablespoons chopped pecans or
   pine nuts
2 tablespoons crumbled
   crisp-cooked bacon
2 tablespoons chopped fresh basil
1/2 cup chopped fresh or
   dried tomatoes
1 (8-count) can crescent rolls

Preheat the oven to 350 degrees.

Cut the Brie into halves horizontally. Layer the pecans, bacon, basil and tomatoes on one half. Place the other Brie piece on top to make a sandwich. Unroll the crescent rolls on a smooth flat surface. Press the perforations together, making a large rectangle. Wrap the Brie in the crescent roll dough to cover.

Bake for 12 to 15 minutes or until golden brown. Serve with crackers or baguette slices.

Serves 12

Try this at the end of the summer when the basil and tomatoes are fresh.

Garlic Pepper Cheese Rounds

8 ounces cream cheese, softened
1/3 cup butter, softened
1/2 cup (2 ounces) freshly grated
   Parmesan cheese
2 to 4 garlic cloves, minced
1/4 teaspoon dried oregano
   Freshly ground pepper

Combine the cream cheese, butter, Parmesan cheese, garlic and oregano in a bowl and mix well. Shape the mixture into two logs.

Place a sheet of waxed paper on a flat surface. Grind some pepper on the waxed paper and roll the logs in the pepper, turning to coat. Wrap the logs in plastic wrap and chill in the refrigerator until firm.

To serve, unwrap the logs and cut into slices. Arrange on a serving platter with toasted baguette slices or assorted crackers.

Variation: Roll the logs in chopped parsley instead of pepper.

Makes 24 rounds

Shiitake Mushroom and Artichoke Dip

10 ounces shiitake mushroom
   caps, sliced
 2 garlic cloves, minced
 1 tablespoon olive oil
16 ounces cream cheese, softened
1/2 cup mayonnaise
 1 (14-ounce) can artichoke hearts,
   drained and coarsely chopped
1/4 cup green onions, chopped
1/4 cup (1 ounce) grated
   Parmesan cheese
 1 teaspoon black pepper
3/4 teaspoon salt
1/4 teaspoon cayenne pepper

Sauté the mushrooms and garlic in the olive oil in a large skillet over medium-high heat for 5 minutes or until tender. Add the cream cheese, mayonnaise, artichoke hearts, green onions, Parmesan cheese, black pepper, salt and cayenne pepper and mix well. Cook over medium heat until heated through, stirring constantly.

Preheat the oven to 350 degrees. Spoon the mushroom mixture into a baking dish coated with nonstick cooking spray. Bake for 30 minutes or until heated through. Serve with crackers, bread and/or fresh vegetables.

Serves 6 to 8

To properly clean a mushroom, use a damp clean cloth or soft bristled brush and gently wipe off the outside. Do not submerge the mushrooms in water; they will absorb the water and will be much less flavorful.

Zesty Blue Cheese Toasts

 8 ounces cream cheese, softened
1/2 cup mayonnaise
1/4 cup minced green onions
 2 ounces blue cheese, crumbled
1/4 teaspoon cayenne pepper
24 thin slices cocktail pumpernickel
   or rye bread
   Paprika
   Pimentos
   Olives

Combine the cream cheese, mayonnaise, green onions, blue cheese and cayenne pepper in a bowl and mix well. Spread 1 tablespoon of the cream cheese mixture on each bread slice. (At this point, you may freeze the toasts. Arrange on a baking sheet and place in the freezer. Once frozen, store the toasts in large sealable plastic bags.)

Preheat the oven to 350 degrees. Arrange the toasts on a baking sheet and sprinkle with paprika. Bake for 15 minutes or until bubbly. Garnish with pimentos and/or olives.

Makes 24 toasts

Lovely Layered Crab Spread

8 ounces cream cheese, softened
1/2 cup sour cream
1/4 cup mayonnaise
2 teaspoons Worcestershire sauce
2 teaspoons minced fresh or dried onion
3/4 cup chunky salsa or chili sauce
8 ounces fresh or canned crab meat, drained and flaked
1 cup (4 ounces) shredded mozzarella cheese
2 green onions, chopped
1 small tomato, chopped

Combine the cream cheese, sour cream, mayonnaise, Worcestershire sauce and onion in a bowl and mix well. Spread the mixture in a 12-inch deep-dish pie plate. Layer the salsa, crab meat, mozzarella cheese, green onions and tomato over the cream cheese mixture and press down slightly. Chill, covered, in the refrigerator until ready to serve. Serve with assorted crackers.

Serves 8 to 10

Fresh crab is easy to find in the Pacific Northwest and makes this appetizer extra-special. See page 125 for an easy way to prepare fresh crab.

The Apple Cup—A Famous Rivalry

The Apple Cup is the annual college football match-up against state rival schools, Washington State University and the University of Washington. The game is played in November and alternates every year from one campus to the other. The game originated in 1900 when the University of Washington tied what was then the Washington Agricultural College. Since then, there have been ninety-eight games (through 2005). Given that Washington is known for its apples, in 1962, the game became appropriately known as the Apple Cup. An Apple Cup trophy has been awarded to the winner every year since. The record as of 2005 is UW sixty-three wins, WSU twenty-nine wins, and six ties. The good-natured rivalry always makes for an exciting game no matter what kind of season the teams are having. The winner takes home the pride, the trophy, and bragging rights for the whole year.

Hot Horsey Crab Spread

8 ounces cream cheese, softened
2 (8-ounce) cans crab meat,
    drained and flaked
1 bunch green onions, chopped
2 tablespoons horseradish
3/4 cup mayonnaise
    Grated Parmesan cheese
    Chopped fresh parsley

Preheat the oven to 325 degrees. Mix the cream cheese, crab meat, green onions, horseradish and mayonnaise in a bowl. Spread the mixture in a pie plate and sprinkle with Pamesan cheese. Bake for 20 minutes or until golden brown and bubbly. Garnish with parsley and serve with crackers or bread rounds.

Makes about 3 cups

Cougar Tailgating Mix

4 cups air-popped popcorn
2 1/2 cups bite-size wheat or bran
    square cereal
1 1/2 cups small pretzels
1 1/2 cups cashews or pecan halves
3/4 cup packed brown sugar
6 tablespoons butter
3 tablespoons light corn syrup
1 teaspoon pumpkin pie spice
1/4 teaspoon baking soda
1/4 teaspoon vanilla extract
1/8 teaspoon ground red pepper

Remove all of the unpopped kernels from the popped popcorn. Mix with the cereal, pretzels and cashews in a 2×2×17-inch baking or roasting pan.

Combine the brown sugar, butter and corn syrup in a medium saucepan and mix well. Cook over medium heat until the mixture boils, stirring constantly with a wooden spoon. Reduce the heat to medium-low. Cook without stirring for 5 minutes longer. Remove from the heat and stir in the pumpkin pie spice, baking soda, vanilla and red pepper. Pour over the popcorn mixture and stir lightly to coat.

Preheat the oven to 300 degrees. Bake for 15 minutes. Stir the mixture and bake for 5 minutes longer. Spread the mixture on a buttered large piece of foil to cool. When completely cool and hardened, break into pieces. Store, tightly covered, for up to 5 to 7 days.

Serves 8 to 10

Apricot Party Punch with a Punch

1 (46-ounce) can apricot nectar
1 (46-ounce) can pineapple juice
1 (12-ounce) can frozen orange
   juice concentrate, thawed
1 (12-ounce) can frozen lemonade
   concentrate, thawed
2 cups apricot brandy
2 cups vodka
   Squirt soda

Combine the apricot nectar, pineapple juice, orange juice concentrate, lemonade concentrate, brandy and vodka in a large sealable plastic container and freeze.

To serve, thaw the frozen mixture slightly, until slushy. Mix 2 parts slush with 1 part Squirt for each serving.

For a nonalcoholic beverage, substitute 4 cups water for the brandy and vodka. Serve over ice.

Serves 10 to 12

"Fall off the Dock" Lemonade

1 shot amaretto
1 shot Absolut Citron vodka
8 ounces pulp-free lemonade

Combine the amaretto, vodka and lemonade in a cocktail shaker with ice. Shake well and pour over ice. For a fun summer alternative, combine the ingredients with ice in a blender and serve frozen.

Makes 1 serving

Madison's Mango Martini

2 parts Malibu Mango rum
1/2 part sweetened lime juice
3 dashes of Angostura bitters

Combine the rum, lime juice and bitters in a cocktail shaker with ice. Shake well and strain into a martini glass. Enjoy!

Makes 1 serving

French Kiss on the Beach

1 ounce vodka
1 ounce peach schnapps
1 ounce blue curaçao
3¹/₂ ounces pineapple juice

Combine the vodka, schnapps, curaçao and pineapple juice in a cocktail shaker half-filled with ice. Shake well, strain into a martini glass and serve.

Makes 1 serving

B&K's Pear Brandy Special

Juice of 1 orange
Juice of ¹/₂ lemon
1 shot Cointreau
1 shot pear brandy
¹/₂ shot limoncello

Mix the orange juice, lemon juice, Cointreau, pear brandy and limoncello in a cocktail shaker with ice. Shake well and strain into a martini glass.

Note: Pear brandy is often made with locally grown fruit. It takes up to 28 pounds of pears to make one large bottle of brandy. (See www.clearcreek distillery.com for more information.)

Makes 1 serving

This one will wow your guests!

Rockin' Rockford Vanilla Lemon Drop

Crystal sugar
1¹/₄ cups fresh lemonade
2 shots Vanilla Stoli vodka
¹/₂ shot Triple Sec
Lemon wedge

Sugar the rim of a martini glass. Combine the lemonade, vodka and Triple Sec in a cocktail shaker with ice. Shake well and strain into the prepared glass. Garnish with a lemon wedge.

Makes 1 serving

Company Wine Cocktail

2/3 cup chilled white wine
1/3 cup crème de cassis
Twist of lemon peel

Combine the wine and the crème de cassis in a wine glass. Garnish with a twist of lemon peel.

Makes 1 serving

Macaulay's Christmas Eggnog

1 1/2 gallons eggnog
1/3 cup rum
1/3 cup spiced rum
1/3 cup Godiva white chocolate
liqueur
Sprinkle of nutmeg

Combine the eggnog, rum, spiced rum and liqueur in a punch bowl and mix well. Sprinkle with nutmeg to serve.

Serves 10 to 12

Grady's Irish Cream

1 pint half-and-half
1 (14-ounce) can sweetened
condensed milk
1 tablespoon Hershey's
chocolate syrup
1 teaspoon vanilla extract
1/2 to 3/4 cup dark rum
1/2 to 3/4 cup whiskey or brandy
2 teaspoons instant coffee granules

Combine the half-and-half, condensed milk, chocolate syrup, vanilla, rum, whiskey and coffee granules in a blender. Process until well blended. Serve in coffee or on the rocks.

This will keep in the refrigerator for about 2 weeks.

Makes 16 servings

Children of the Sun

BRUNCH, BREAKFAST & BREADS

Chapter Sponsor: *Great Harvest Bread Company*

A rainbow arches up the Spokane Falls under the Monroe Street Bridge.
Photograph courtesy of The Spokesman-Review.

Mushroom and Pepper Quiche

1 teaspoon butter or margarine
1½ cups chopped onions
1 red bell pepper, chopped
4 ounces domestic or wild mushrooms, minced
½ teaspoon salt
½ teaspoon pepper
½ teaspoon fresh thyme leaves
½ teaspoon dry mustard
4 eggs
1½ cups milk
2 tablespoons all-purpose flour
1½ cups (6 ounces) packed shredded Swiss cheese
1 unbaked (10-inch) pie shell
Paprika

Preheat the oven to 375 degrees. Melt the butter in a saucepan over medium heat. Add the onions and bell pepper. Sauté until tender. Add the mushrooms, salt, pepper, thyme and mustard. Cook for 5 minutes longer, stirring frequently. Remove from the heat.

Beat the eggs, milk and flour in a large mixing bowl until smooth.

Spread the cheese over the bottom of the pie shell. Layer the mushroom mixture over the cheese. Pour the egg mixture over the top and sprinkle with paprika. Bake for 35 to 45 minutes or until set in the center. Serve hot, warm or at room temperature.

Serves 4 to 6

Chanterelle mushrooms are native to the Northwest and are very tasty!

Lilac Festival and Torchlight Parade

Spokane and Fairchild Air Force Base are very much a community together, and that is never more evident than every spring during the Armed Forces Torchlight Parade, the culmination of the Lilac Festival. This annual parade continues to delight young and old, drawing crowds year after year. A highlight of the parade, going back to its beginning, is the selection of the Lilac Festival Royal Court. Applicants are chosen from surrounding Spokane County high schools. Young women selected for the Royal Court receive scholarships for college and represent the greater Spokane area in a variety of events. The Spokane Lilac Festival and Armed Forces Torchlight Parade honor our nation's military, offer fun parade floats and lovely princesses, and provide entertainment for all ages.

Chicken and Salsa Quiche

3/4 cup diced red bell pepper
1 cup (4 ounces) shredded
   Cheddar cheese
1 cup (4 ounces) shredded
   Swiss cheese
1 cup chopped cooked chicken
1 unbaked (9-inch) deep-dish
   pie shell
2 tablespoons butter
1/2 cup chopped onion
1 tablespoon all-purpose flour
1/2 cup half-and-half
1/2 cup sour cream
4 eggs, beaten
   Salsa

Preheat the oven to 350 degrees. Layer the bell pepper, Cheddar cheese, Swiss cheese and chicken in the pie shell. Melt the butter in a skillet over medium heat. Add the onion. Sauté for 4 minutes or until tender. Stir in the flour and mix well. Add the half-and-half. Simmer for 3 to 5 minutes or until thickened, stirring constantly. Let cool.

Combine the sour cream and eggs in a bowl and mix well. Stir into the onion mixture. Pour the filling into the pie shell. Bake for 35 to 40 minutes or until set. Serve with salsa.

Serves 4 to 6

Christmas Morning Eggs

2 cups (8 ounces) shredded
   Cheddar cheese
1 (10-ounce) package frozen
   spinach, thawed and drained
8 ounces ham, cubed
1 tablespoon butter
6 ounces mushrooms, sliced
1/2 cup chopped green onions
12 eggs, lightly beaten
2 cups heavy cream
1 cup (4 ounces) shredded
   Swiss cheese
   Paprika

Preheat the oven to 350 degrees. Layer the Cheddar cheese, spinach and ham in a greased 9×13-inch baking dish. Melt the butter in a skillet. Add the mushrooms and green onions. Sauté until tender. Spread the mixture over the ham. Beat the eggs and cream in a large mixing bowl. Pour over the ingredients in the baking dish. Top with the Swiss cheese and sprinkle with paprika. Bake for 30 minutes or until set.

Serves 12

The whole dish can be prepared and baked in advance and refrigerated, then reheated before serving.

Sausage and Apples

2 (10-count) packages
   breakfast sausage links
2 Granny Smith apples
2 Gala apples
2 Golden Delicious apples
   Brown sugar
   Ground cinnamon

Brown the sausages in a skillet. Remove from the heat and let cool slightly. Chill, covered, in the refrigerator overnight.

Preheat the oven to 350 degrees. Peel and cut the apples into 1-inch wedges. Alternate layers of apples and sausages in a 9×13-inch baking dish, beginning and ending with apples. Sprinkle generously with brown sugar and cinnamon. Bake for 30 minutes, stirring after 15 minutes.

Serves 8 to 10

Washington Apples

More than half of all apples grown in the United States for eating come from Washington state orchards. The Red Delicious is the most widely grown, but there are many other varieties such as Jonagold, Cameo, and Golden Delicious. There are no harvesting machines to pick apples—they must all be picked by hand!

Fresh Mushroom, Bacon and Egg Puff

4 cups cubed dry white bread or
French bread
2 cups (8 ounces) shredded
Cheddar cheese
4 cups milk
10 eggs, lightly beaten
1 teaspoon dry mustard
1/4 teaspoon onion powder
1 teaspoon salt
1/8 teaspoon freshly ground pepper
10 slices bacon, crisp-cooked
and crumbled
1/2 cup chopped tomatoes
1/2 cup sliced fresh mushrooms

Arrange the bread in a generously buttered 9×13-inch baking dish.
Sprinkle evenly with the cheese. Beat the eggs, milk, mustard, onion
powder, salt and pepper in a large bowl until well blended. Pour over the
cheese. Sprinkle with the bacon, tomatoes and mushrooms. Chill,
covered, in the refrigerator for 8 hours or longer.

Preheat the oven to 325 degrees. Bake, uncovered, for 1 hour or until set.
Tent with foil if the top becomes too brown.

Note: This recipe must be started a day ahead so that it can spend at least
8 hours in the refrigerator.

Serves 8 to 10

Orange Upside-Down French Toast

1/4 cup (1/2 stick) butter
1/3 cup sugar
1/4 teaspoon ground cinnamon
1 teaspoon grated orange zest
4 eggs, lightly beaten
2/3 cup orange juice
8 thick slices, firm white or
whole wheat bread

Preheat the oven to 400 degrees. Melt the butter in a 10×15-inch baking
pan in the oven. Combine the sugar, cinnamon and orange zest in a small
bowl and mix well. Sprinkle evenly in the pan. Whisk the eggs and orange
juice in a shallow bowl until blended. Dip the bread into the egg mixture,
allowing it to become saturated. Arrange the bread in the pan and spoon
any remaining egg mixture over the bread. Bake for 25 minutes. Let stand
for 2 minutes. Remove to a hot platter, sugar side up.

Serves 8

Sausage Phyllo Breakfast Strudels

1½ tablespoons unsalted
butter, melted
1½ tablespoons all-purpose flour
¾ cup milk
6 tablespoons shredded
Gruyère cheese
2 tablespoons grated
Parmesan cheese
¼ teaspoon salt
⅛ teaspoon cayenne pepper
Nutmeg to taste
4 ounces bulk pork sausage
5 eggs
1½ teaspoons minced fresh thyme, or
½ teaspoon dried thyme
¼ teaspoon salt
Black pepper to taste
1 tablespoon butter
1 tablespoon minced fresh parsley
½ cup (1 stick) butter, melted
6 thick sheets phyllo dough

Combine 1½ tablespoons of the butter with the flour in a small saucepan over medium-high heat. Cook for 3 minutes, stirring constantly. Whisk in the milk gradually. Bring to a boil. Cook for 2 to 3 minutes or until the mixture thickens, whisking constantly. Remove from the heat. Stir in the cheeses gradually. Stir in ¼ teaspoon salt and the cayenne pepper. Season generously with nutmeg. Pour the mixture into a large bowl and set aside. Brown the sausage in a skillet, stirring until crumbly. Drain on paper towels.

Combine the eggs, thyme, ¼ teaspoon salt and black pepper in a medium bowl and mix well. Add the sausage and mix well. Heat 1 tablespoon butter in a skillet over medium heat. Add the egg mixture. Cook just until set but still moist, stirring constantly. Add the egg mixture to the cheese sauce. Add the parsley and mix well. Let cool.

Preheat the oven to 375 degrees. Brush a rimmed baking sheet with some of the ½ cup melted butter. Arrange one phyllo sheet on a clean kitchen towel on a smooth work surface. (Keep the other sheets covered with a damp towel.) Brush the phyllo generously with the remaining melted butter. Fold the sheet into halves lengthwise and brush again with butter.

Spoon ⅓ cup of the filling on the short end of the phyllo nearest you. Spread the filling horizontally in a 3-inch wide strip, leaving a ¾-inch border on the long edges. Fold the edges of the two long sides of the pastry over the filling, tucking the short ends under to form a packet. Place the packet seam side down on the prepared baking sheet. Brush the top with butter. Repeat with the remaining phyllo sheets and filling. Bake the strudels for 15 minutes or until golden brown.

Serves 6

Try this with Greenbluff Strawberry Spinach Salad (page 76) and Incredibly Good Blueberry Muffins (page 56) for a special spring brunch.

Suzette Butter Crepes

Crepes

    4 eggs
       Pinch of salt
    2 tablespoons sugar
 1/2 teaspoon vanilla extract
1 1/2 cups milk
    1 cup all-purpose flour
    2 tablespoons butter
       Melted butter for cooking

Suzette Butter

    2 oranges
    2 (1/2×1-inch) strips lemon peel
 2/3 cup sugar
   10 tablespoons butter, softened
    4 tablespoons orange curaçao

To Serve

    2 tablespoons orange curaçao
    2 tablespoons brandy, heated

For the crepes, combine the eggs, salt, sugar and vanilla in a blender. Cover and process at low speed for 5 seconds. Add the milk in a fine stream, processing constantly until smooth. Add the flour slowly through a funnel, processing constantly until smooth. Melt 2 tablespoons butter in a 6-inch crepe pan or cast-iron skillet over medium-high heat. Add the butter to the blender slowly, processing constantly until smooth.

Spread a small amount of melted butter evenly over the hot crepe pan. Pour in 2 tablespoons batter. Tilt the pan quickly so the batter will spread evenly over the pan. Cook the crepe until brown on the bottom. Turn and cook the other side. Remove to a plate, second cooked side up. Wipe the crepe pan with lightly buttered cheesecloth and repeat the process with the remaining batter. Cover the stacked crepes with plastic wrap until ready to use.

For the Suzette Butter, use a vegetable peeler to remove the colored portion of the orange peel. Juice the oranges into a small bowl. Combine the orange peel, lemon peel and orange juice in a blender. Cover and process until the peel is finely chopped. Add the sugar, butter and curaçao. Cover and process at high speed until blended. Pour the mixture into a small bowl. Chill, covered, in the refrigerator until ready to use.

To serve, melt half the Suzette Butter in a chafing dish or skillet. Heat one crepe at a time in the sauce. Turn to heat both sides. Remove to a plate, second cooked side down. (This will provide better color when the crepe is folded.) Use a fork and spoon to fold the crepes into quarters after cooking. Top with Suzette Butter as needed. Set the folded crepes around the edge of the pan with the folded corners all facing the same direction.

When ready to serve, spoon the curaçao and brandy over twelve crepes. Immediately touch with a flame to ignite. Baste with the sauce to keep the flame burning. Tip the pan if needed to coat with sauce. This is delicious for dessert, as well as for brunch.

Serves 12 (with extra crepes)

Wonderful Waffles

2 egg whites
2 cups all-purpose flour
4 teaspoons baking powder
1/2 teaspoon salt
2 tablespoons sugar
1 teaspoon ground cinnamon
1 teaspoon nutmeg
13/4 cups milk
2 egg yolks, beaten
1/2 cup (1 stick) butter, melted

Preheat the waffle iron. Beat the egg whites in a mixing bowl with an electric mixer until stiff peaks form. Whisk the dry ingredients in a large bowl. Add the milk, egg yolks and butter gradually, beating well after each addition. Fold in the egg whites. Cook the waffles using the manufacturer's instructions.

Variation: Try these with homemade applesauce for a yummy and healthy twist!

Serves 6 to 8

German Oven Pancake

4 eggs
1 cup milk
1 teaspoon vanilla extract
1 cup all-purpose flour
1/4 teaspoon salt
1 teaspoon sugar
1 tablespoon butter
Confectioners' sugar
for sprinkling
Lemon juice (optional)
Warm syrup (optional)
Jam (optional)
Sliced fruit (optional)

Preheat the oven to 450 degrees. Beat the eggs in a mixing bowl until foamy. Beat in the milk and vanilla until smooth. Add the flour, salt and sugar, beating until smooth.

Melt the butter in a 10- or 12-inch skillet or 9×13-inch baking dish in the oven. When the butter is melted and very hot, pour the batter into the skillet and return it to the oven. Bake for 15 minutes or until golden brown and puffy.

Sprinkle with confectioners' sugar. Cut into slices and serve with lemon juice, warm syrup, jam, or sliced fruit.

Serves 4

Oven-Baked French Toast

1/4 cup (1/2 stick) butter
2 tablespoons honey
1/2 teaspoon ground cinnamon
3 eggs
1/2 cup orange juice
1/8 teaspoon salt
6 slices bread
   Confectioners' sugar (optional)

Preheat the oven to 400 degrees. Melt the butter with the honey in a saucepan over medium heat. Spread the mixture over the bottom of a 9×13-inch baking dish and sprinkle with the cinnamon. Beat the eggs, orange juice and salt in a mixing bowl until smooth. Soak each slice of bread in the egg mixture. Arrange the bread in the baking dish. Bake for 20 minutes. Dust with confectioners' sugar before serving.

Serves 4 to 6

Children of the Sun

According to author David Wynecoop, it is generally accepted that "the word 'Spokane' means 'sun people' or 'people of the sun'" (Children of the Sun by David Wynecoop). The group enjoyed the crystal clear waters of the Spokane River, where salmon teemed. They lived in harmony with the change of seasons. One can see why the Spokane Indian Tribe, part of a larger group of Native Americans, the Interior Salish Group, lived and thrived in the area of Spokane and parts of Idaho and Montana for hundreds of years. Things that are still appreciated in Spokane today, berries, fishing, and wild game, were important then, too.

Multigrain Pancakes

Oat Blend

1³/₄ cups rolled oats
¹/₄ cup whole wheat flour
¹/₄ cup buttermilk powder
3 tablespoons oat bran or plain bran cereal
2 tablespoons sugar

Pancakes

³/₄ cup all-purpose flour
1¹/₂ teaspoons baking powder
¹/₄ teaspoon salt
1 cup water
3 tablespoons vegetable oil
2 eggs

For the oat blend, combine the oats, whole wheat flour, buttermilk powder, oat bran and sugar in a blender or food processor. Process until the oats are ground and the mixture is well blended.

For the pancakes, measure ³/₄ cup of the oat mixture into a bowl. (Freeze the remaining oat mixture for later use.) Add the flour, baking powder and salt and mix well. Whisk the water, oil and eggs in a bowl until blended. Add the dry ingredients to the egg mixture, stirring just until combined. (Don't worry about small lumps.) Let stand for 5 minutes.

Drop ¹/₄ cupfuls of batter onto a hot greased griddle or skillet. Cook until bubbles appear on the surface and the underside is golden. Turn and cook the other side.

Makes 12 pancakes

Homemade Applesauce

Zest and juice of 2 large navel oranges
Zest and juice of 1 lemon
3 pounds Granny Smith apples
3 pounds sweet red apples, such as McIntosh or Winesap
¹/₂ cup packed light brown sugar
¹/₂ cup (1 stick) unsalted butter
2 teaspoons ground cinnamon
¹/₂ teaspoon ground allspice

Preheat the oven to 350 degrees. Combine the zests and juices of the oranges and lemon in a large bowl. Peel, core and quarter the apples and place in the bowl. Toss the apples with the juices and zest. Pour the mixture into a Dutch oven. Add the brown sugar, butter, cinnamon and allspice and mix well. Bake, covered, for 1¹/₂ hours or until the apples are tender, stirring occasionally. Whisk until the applesauce is smooth. Serve warm over pancakes.

Makes 8 to 10 cups

Huckleberry Bread

Bread

- 1/3 cup melted butter
- 3/4 cup sugar
- 2 tablespoons grated lemon zest
- 3 tablespoons fresh lemon juice
- 2 eggs
- 1 1/2 cups sifted all-purpose flour
- 1 teaspoon baking powder
- 1 teaspoon salt
- 1/2 cup milk
- 1/2 cup chopped walnuts or macadamia nuts
- 1 cup frozen huckleberries tossed with 1 tablespoon all-purpose flour

Glaze

- 1 tablespoon heavy cream or milk
- 2 tablespoons grated lemon zest (optional)
- 1 tablespoon lemon juice
- 1/2 cup sifted confectioners' sugar

For the bread, preheat the oven to 350 degrees. Combine the butter, sugar, lemon zest and lemon juice in a large bowl and mix well. Beat in the eggs. Combine the flour, baking powder and salt in a bowl and mix well. Add the flour mixture to the butter mixture alternately with the milk, ending with the flour mixture. Fold in the walnuts and huckleberries. Spoon the mixture into a large greased loaf pan or three miniature loaf pans. Bake for 1 hour. Cool in the pan for 10 minutes. Remove to a wire rack set over waxed paper.

For the glaze, combine the cream, lemon zest, lemon juice and confectioners' sugar in a small bowl and mix well. Drizzle over the bread.

Makes 1 large loaf or 3 miniature loaves

Huckleberries

Found growing wild in the Pacific Northwest and treasured for their strong sweet and tart taste, the huckleberry is a regional favorite. Huckleberry hunters must be both skilled and patient to find the elusive berries, which have not been domesticated (although efforts are being made to do so, to the dismay of purists). By mid- to late summer, the berries are also available for purchase at better grocery stores and markets, for those who do not wish to join the hunt. In recipes that call for huckleberries, blueberries can be substituted in a pinch.

Huckleberry Coffee Cake

1/4 cup (1/2 stick) margarine, softened
4 ounces fat-free cream cheese, softened
1 cup sugar
1 egg
1 cup all-purpose flour
1 teaspoon baking powder
1/4 teaspoon salt
1 teaspoon vanilla extract
2 cups huckleberries or blueberries

Preheat the oven to 350 degrees. Beat the margarine and cream cheese in a bowl with a mixer at medium speed until fluffy. Beat in the sugar gradually. Add the egg and beat well. Combine the flour, baking powder and salt in a small bowl. Stir into the margarine mixture. Stir in the vanilla. Fold in the huckleberries. Pour into a 9-inch round baking pan sprayed with nonstick cooking spray. Bake for 1 hour. Let cool slightly before serving.

Serves 10

Wonderful with strawberries!

Island Banana Bread

1¹/4 cups all-purpose flour
1 cup sugar
1/2 teaspoon salt
1 teaspoon baking soda
1/2 cup (1 stick) butter, softened
3 bananas, mashed
2 eggs, beaten
3/4 cup chopped pecans
3/4 cup flaked coconut

Preheat the oven to 350 degrees. Combine the flour, sugar, salt and baking soda in a medium bowl and mix well. Combine the butter, bananas and eggs in a bowl, stirring until well blended. Add the flour mixture and mix well. Stir in the pecans and coconut. Spoon the mixture into two greased loaf pans. Bake for 45 minutes.

Makes 2 loaves

A taste of the sun—perfect for a chilly winter day!

Rhubarb Bread

2¹/₄ cups packed brown sugar
1 cup vegetable oil
2 eggs
1¹/₂ cups buttermilk
1 teaspoon vanilla extract
1¹/₂ teaspoons salt
1¹/₂ teaspoons baking soda
3³/₄ cups all-purpose flour
2¹/₄ cups chopped rhubarb
1 cup nuts, chopped
¹/₂ cup packed brown sugar
1 tablespoon margarine

Preheat the oven to 325 degrees. Beat 2¹/₄ cups brown sugar and the oil in a bowl until well blended. Add the eggs and mix well. Beat in the buttermilk and vanilla. Combine the salt, baking soda and flour in a bowl and mix well. Stir the flour mixture into the oil mixture, mixing just until no dry streaks of flour remain. Fold in the rhubarb and nuts. Spoon into two greased loaf pans. Combine ¹/₂ cup brown sugar and the margarine in a bowl, stirring until crumbly. Sprinkle over the batter. Bake for 40 to 50 minutes.

Makes 2 loaves

French Breakfast Popovers

Popovers
¹/₂ cup sugar
¹/₃ cup shortening
1 egg
1¹/₂ cups all-purpose flour
¹/₂ teaspoon baking powder
¹/₂ teaspoon salt
¹/₄ teaspoon ground nutmeg
¹/₂ cup milk

Topping
¹/₂ cup sugar
1 teaspoon ground cinnamon
6 tablespoons butter, melted

Preheat the oven to 350 degrees.

For the popovers, beat the sugar and shortening in a mixing bowl until fluffy. Add the egg and mix well. Combine the flour, baking powder, salt and nutmeg in a bowl and mix well. Add the flour mixture to the sugar mixture alternately with the milk, beating well after each addition. Spoon the mixture into twelve greased muffin cups, filling each cup two-thirds full. Bake for 20 to 25 minutes.

For the topping, combine the sugar and cinnamon in a small bowl. Remove the popovers from the muffin cups. Dip the popovers into the butter, then into the cinnamon-sugar.

Makes 12 popovers

Buttermilk Scones

Scones

- 3 cups all-purpose flour
- 1/3 cup sugar
- 2 1/2 teaspoons baking powder
- 1/2 teaspoon baking soda
- 3/4 teaspoon salt
- 3/4 cup (1 1/2 sticks) butter, chilled
- 1 cup buttermilk
- 3/4 cup currants
- 1 teaspoon grated orange zest

Cinnamon Glaze

- 1 tablespoon heavy cream
- 1/4 teaspoon ground cinnamon
- 2 tablespoons sugar

Preheat the oven to 425 degrees.

For the scones, combine the flour, sugar, baking powder, baking soda and salt in a mixing bowl and mix well with a fork. Cut in the butter with a pastry blender or two knives or work in with your fingertips until the mixture resembles fresh bread crumbs. Add the buttermilk, currants and orange zest. Mix just until the dry ingredients are moistened. Gather the dough into a ball and press so it holds together. Turn the dough onto a lightly floured surface. Knead lightly twelve times. Pat the dough into a circle 1/2 inch thick.

For the glaze, combine the cream, cinnamon and sugar in a small bowl and mix well. Brush the dough with the glaze. Cut the dough into eighteen wedges and arrange on a baking sheet. Bake for 12 minutes or until the tops are browned. Serve hot with Mock Devon Cream.

Makes 18 scones

Mock Devon Cream

- 3 ounces cream cheese, softened
- 1 tablespoon confectioners' sugar
- 1/2 teaspoon vanilla extract
- 1/3 to 1/2 cup heavy cream

Beat the cream cheese in a mixing bowl with an electric mixer until light and fluffy. Beat in the confectioners' sugar and vanilla. Gradually beat in enough cream until the mixture is of a spreading consistency; do not overbeat. Chill, covered, in the refrigerator for 2 to 24 hours.

Makes about 1 cup

English Tea Scones

1 egg, lightly beaten
  Buttermilk
2 cups all-purpose flour
1/4 cup sugar
2 1/2 teaspoons baking powder
1/2 teaspoon salt
6 tablespoons butter
1/2 cup raisins, sweetened dried
  cranberries, blueberries or
  chopped dried apricots
1/2 cup white chocolate chips
  (optional)

Preheat the oven to 400 degrees. Break the egg into a 1-cup measure. Add enough buttermilk to equal 1 cup; set aside.

Combine the flour, sugar, baking powder and salt in a large mixing bowl and mix well. Cut in the butter until the mixture resembles coarse crumbs. Stir in the dried fruit and white chocolate chips. Add the dry ingredients to the buttermilk mixture. Stir until the dough holds together.

Drop the dough a scant 1/4 cup at a time onto an ungreased baking sheet. Bake for 12 to 15 minutes or until golden brown.

Makes 12 large scones

Lemon Curd

2 pounds young zucchini
1/2 cup (1 stick) butter
3 cups sugar
  Grated zest and juice of
  3 large lemons
2 packets liquid pectin

Peel and slice the zucchini and place in a 3-quart pan with enough water to cover. Bring to a boil over high heat. Reduce the heat and simmer for 20 minutes or until tender. Remove from the heat and drain. Let cool for 15 minutes.

Purée the zucchini in a blender or food processor or mash by hand. Combine the zucchini purée, butter and sugar in a 5-quart pan. Add the lemon zest and lemon juice and mix well. Bring to a full boil, stirring constantly. Add the pectin and mix well. Boil for 3 minutes. Remove from the heat. Pour the mixture into six sterilized 1/2-pint jars.

Seal the jars. Cool for 30 minutes at room temperature. Lemon curd can be stored for 2 weeks in the refrigerator or indefinitely in the freezer.

Makes six 1/2-pint jars

Harvest Scones

Scones

- 4 cups (or more) all-purpose flour
- 4 teaspoons baking powder
- 3/4 cup sugar
- 1 teaspoon salt
  Grated zest of 1 orange
- 1 cup (2 sticks) butter, softened and cut into small pieces
- 2 eggs
- 1/3 cup frozen orange juice concentrate
- 1/3 cup milk
- 1/2 cup sweetened dried cranberries or fresh cranberries

Glaze

- 1/2 cup confectioners' sugar
- 2 tablespoons orange juice

Preheat the oven to 375 degrees.

For the scones, combine the flour, baking powder, sugar, salt and orange zest in a bowl and mix well. Cut in the butter until the mixture resembles coarse crumbs. Whisk the eggs, orange juice concentrate and milk in a small bowl. Set aside 2 to 3 tablespoons of the egg mixture to brush over the scones before baking. Stir the remaining egg mixture into the flour mixture, mixing just until moistened. If the dough is too sticky to handle, add a little more flour. Fold in the cranberries. Turn the dough onto a floured surface. Knead a few times to form a ball. Divide the dough into two equal portions. Pat each portion into a circle about 1 inch thick. Cut each circle into six wedges. Arrange on a greased baking sheet and brush with the reserved egg mixture. Bake for 20 to 25 minutes or just until golden brown. Remove to a wire rack set over a sheet of waxed paper.

For the glaze, combine the confectioners' sugar and orange juice in a small bowl and mix well. Drizzle in a zigzag pattern across the cooling scones.

Makes 12 scones

The Spokanes and the First European Settlers

As with so many Native American tribes, the appearance of white settlers after 1807 in the Spokane area marked the beginning of a struggle for survival. The population, once estimated at three thousand, was recorded in 1897 as "340 Lower Spokanes" and "188 Upper and Middle Spokanes." The Homestead Act, passed in 1862, steadily eroded the tribal lands. Still, they persevered.

Cheddar Dill Scones

2 cups all-purpose flour
1 tablespoon baking powder
1 teaspoon kosher salt
6 tablespoons cold unsalted
   butter, diced
1 cup (4 ounces) sharp Cheddar
   cheese, shredded
1 teaspoon dried dill weed
2 eggs, lightly beaten
1/2 cup heavy cream or light cream
1 egg, beaten with
   1 tablespoon water

Preheat the oven to 400 degrees. Combine the flour, baking powder and salt in a food processor (or beat with an electric mixer set at low speed). Add the butter and process until crumbly. Stir in the cheese and dill weed.

Whisk the eggs and cream in a small bowl until blended. Add to the flour mixture and mix until just combined. Turn the dough onto a well-floured surface and knead for 1 minute or until the cheese and dill weed are evenly distributed. Roll the dough into a circle 3/4 inch thick. Cut into eight wedges and arrange on a baking sheet lined with baking parchment. Brush the tops with the egg mixture. Bake for 20 to 30 minutes.

Makes 8 scones

The Spokane Today

The Spokane Tribe would triumph over disease, bigotry, and overwhelming social change. Today there are "1,909 enrolled Spokane tribal members," and the Reservation is home to an elementary school, high school, museum, library, and health center. The Tribe hosts an annual celebration each Labor Day weekend with "traditional Indian dancing, stick games, and dancing contests," as well as crafts, trading, and sales. Healthy revenues from various businesses keep the Tribe on sound financial footing, and their generosity to the Spokane community is great.

The Spokane Tribe is as much a part of Spokane as the river itself. Just as people now recognize the intrinsic value and beauty that the Spokane River holds, they have also come to appreciate the great people and culture that first settled the Inland Northwest. We are grateful that we can enter the future together in this remarkable place we all call our home.

Incredibly Good Blueberry Muffins

2 cups all-purpose flour
1 cup sugar
2 teaspoons baking powder
1/2 teaspoon salt
1/2 cup milk
1/2 cup (1 stick) lightly salted butter,
  melted and cooled
1 egg, lightly beaten
1 teaspoon vanilla extract
2 cups fresh or frozen blueberries,
  tossed with 1 tablespoon
  all-purpose flour
1 tablespoon sugar

Preheat the oven to 400 degrees. Combine the flour, 1 cup sugar, the baking powder and salt in a large bowl. Whisk the milk, butter, egg and vanilla in a bowl until blended. Make a well in the center of the dry ingredients. Pour the milk mixture slowly into the well and stir just until combined. Fold in the blueberries.

Spoon the batter into twelve greased muffin cups. Sprinkle the batter with 1 tablespoon sugar. Bake for 20 to 25 minutes or until a wooden pick inserted in the center of a muffin comes out clean. Let cool in the pan on a wire rack for 5 minutes. Remove the muffins from the pan and cool completely. Store in an airtight container. These muffins freeze well.

Makes 12 muffins

Chocolate Chip Pumpkin Muffins

1 cup all-purpose flour
1 cup sugar
1 teaspoon baking powder
1/4 teaspoon baking soda
1/4 teaspoon salt
1/4 teaspoon ground cinnamon
2 eggs, beaten
1 cup canned pumpkin
1/2 cup vegetable oil
1/2 cup pecans, chopped
1/3 cup miniature semisweet
  chocolate chips
3 tablespoons sugar
1 teaspoon ground cinnamon

Preheat the oven to 350 degrees.

Combine the flour, 1 cup sugar, the baking powder, baking soda, salt and 1/4 teaspoon cinnamon in a medium bowl. Combine the eggs, pumpkin and oil in a bowl and mix well. Make a well in the dry ingredients. Pour the pumpkin mixture into the well slowly, stirring just until blended. Fold in the pecans and chocolate chips. Spoon the batter into fifteen greased 2 1/2-inch muffin cups, filling each 2/3 full. Combine 3 tablespoons sugar and 1 teaspoon cinnamon and sprinkle over the batter. Bake for 20 to 25 minutes.

Makes 15 muffins

Cranberry and Oat Muffins

2 cups buttermilk
1 cup old-fashioned rolled oats
1 cup sweetened dried cranberries
1²/3 cups whole wheat flour
2 teaspoons ground nutmeg
1 teaspoon baking soda
1 teaspoon baking powder
1 egg
1 egg white
2 tablespoons canola oil
1/2 cup packed brown sugar
1 cup currants
1/4 cup granulated sugar
1 teaspoon ground cinnamon

Combine the buttermilk, oats and cranberries in a large bowl. Let stand for 30 minutes to plump the cranberries and moisten the oats.

Preheat the oven to 400 degrees. Coat eighteen standard muffin cups with nonstick cooking spray. Sift the flour, nutmeg, baking soda and baking powder into a medium bowl.

Add the egg, egg white, canola oil, brown sugar and currants to the buttermilk mixture and mix well. Add the flour mixture and stir just until blended. Spoon the batter into the prepared cups, filling each 3/4 full.

Combine the granulated sugar and cinnamon in a small bowl and mix well. Sprinkle evenly over the batter. Bake for 15 minutes or until a wooden pick inserted in the center of a muffin comes out clean. Let cool in the pan for 5 minutes. Remove the muffins from the pan and cool completely.

Makes 18 muffins

The Palouse

The Palouse is a unique and beautiful stretch of farmland in the Inland Northwest consisting of rolling hills with rich soil. The traditional crop in the area is winter wheat, so called because it is planted in October and harvested in the summer. The slight freezing of the young wheat plants actually encourages more growth.

Aunt Betty's Dinner Rolls

2 cups milk, scalded
1/2 cup (1 stick) margarine
1 1/2 teaspoons salt
1 cup sugar
2 envelopes dry yeast
1/2 cup warm water
2 eggs, beaten
8 to 9 cups all-purpose flour

Combine the milk, margarine, salt and sugar in a large bowl, stirring until blended. Let cool until no longer hot to the touch. Dissolve the yeast in the water in a large mixing bowl until foamy. Add the yeast mixture to the milk mixture and mix well. Whisk in the eggs until blended. Add half of the flour and beat well. Add enough of the remaining flour to make a dough that is soft but not sticky. Place the dough in a greased bowl, turning to grease the top. Let rise until doubled in bulk. Punch down and let rise again. Preheat the oven to 375 degrees. Shape the dough into rolls and arrange on a greased baking sheet. Let rise until puffy. Bake for 20 minutes.

Makes 48 rolls

Caramel Pecan Rolls

1/2 cup (1 stick) butter
1 cup packed brown sugar
1/2 cup light corn syrup
1/3 cup cream or evaporated milk
1 cup chopped pecans or walnuts
1 recipe Aunt Betty's Dinner
Rolls dough
Butter to taste, softened
Granulated sugar to taste
Brown sugar to taste
Cinnamon to taste
Raisins to taste (optional)

Preheat the oven to 350 degrees. Combine 1/2 cup butter, 1 cup brown sugar, the corn syrup and cream in a saucepan. Cook over medium-low heat until the brown sugar is dissolved and the butter is melted, stirring occasionally. Stir in the pecans. Pour evenly over the bottom of a 9×13-inch baking pan.

Roll the dough into a 1/2-inch-thick rectangle on a lightly floured surface. Spread softened butter in a generous layer over the dough. Sprinkle granulated sugar, brown sugar, cinnamon and raisins evenly over the butter. Roll to enclose the filling, starting at the long end. Press to seal the seam. Cut the tube into 1/2-inch-wide pieces. Arrange the pieces in a single layer over the pecan mixture in the pan. Let stand until the rolls are doubled in bulk.

Bake for 25 minutes. Let stand for 15 minutes. Invert onto foil.

Makes 24 rolls

Honey Wheat Rolls

2 tablespoons yeast
1 teaspoon sugar
1/2 cup warm water
2 eggs, beaten
1/2 cup vegetable oil
1/2 cup honey
1 teaspoon salt
1/2 cup sweetened condensed milk
1/2 cup hot water
3 to 4 cups whole wheat flour

Combine the yeast, sugar and 1/2 cup warm water in a small bowl and mix well. Combine the eggs, oil, honey, salt, condensed milk and 1/2 cup hot water in a large bowl and mix well. Add the yeast mixture and mix well. Stir in the flour gradually, mixing well after each addition. Let the dough rest for 10 to 15 minutes.

Knead the dough and let rise. Punch the dough down and knead again. Let rise again until doubled in bulk. Shape the dough into rolls and arrange on a greased baking sheet. Let rise until puffy.

Preheat the oven to 350 degrees. Bake for 20 to 25 minutes.

Makes about 36 rolls

Spokane Bread

1 cup mayonnaise (not low-fat)
1 cup (4 ounces) grated Parmesan cheese
2 cups chopped green onions (green part only)
1 teaspoon Worcestershire sauce
1 loaf French bread, cut into halves lengthwise

Combine the mayonnaise, cheese, green onions and Worcestershire sauce in a medium bowl and mix well. Arrange the bread on a baking sheet and spread the cheese mixture over the bread. Broil until golden brown and bubbly. Cut into serving pieces.

Serves 10

The perfect bread to accompany all kinds of meat. Try it with dry-rubbed baby back ribs with molasses barbecue sauce.

Fresh from the Northwest

SOUPS, SALADS & SIDES

Artichoke Soup with Parmesan
62

Cuban Black Bean Soup
62

White Chili
63

Cougar Gold, Apple and
Onion Soup
64

Ultimate Comfort Chicken
Noodle Soup
65

Spicy Lentil Soup
66

Chilled Alderwood-Smoked
Salmon Bisque
66

Pea and Pesto Soup
67

Northwestern Wild
Mushroom Soup
67

Warming Winter
Squash Soup
68

Sausage Tortellini Soup
69

Pumpkin Soup
69

"Don't Kiss Me in the
Morning" Caesar Salad
70

Corn Salad with Cilantro
Jalapeño Dressing
70

Curried Chicken Salad
Lettuce Wraps
71

Davenport Hotel's Crab Louis
71

Autumn in Spokane Salad
72

Summery Asian Vermicelli
73

Mediterranean Pasta Salad
74

Northwestern Salad with
Apple and Cheddar
75

Spokane Blue Spinach Salad
75

Greenbluff Strawberry
Spinach Salad
76

Zesty Spinach Salad
76

Super Slaw with Peanut
Dressing
77

Wonderful Watermelon Salad
77

Topper's Greek Salad
78

Huckleberry Poppy Seed
Dressing
78

Washington Apple, Potato,
Onion Gratin
79

Sweet and Spicy Carrots
79

Spicy Corn on the Cob
80

Norwegian Cucumbers
80

Italian Green Beans
81

Green Beans with
Potatoes and Tomatoes
81

Easy Sweet Onions
82

Sweet Onion Rings
82

Mashed Potatoes and Parsnips
83

Red Potatoes Skewers with
Dijon Mustard
83

Sweet Potato Fries
84

Great Grilled Vegetables
84

Coconut and Lime Rice
85

Barley Nut Pilaf
85

The Crab Louis is the Palm Court's signature dish at The Davenport Hotel.
Photograph courtesy of The Spokesman-Review.

Artichoke Soup with Parmesan

1 cup diced white onion
1/4 cup olive oil
10 small artichokes, trimmed, or
2 (14-ounce) cans artichoke
bottoms, drained and chopped
Sea salt and freshly ground
pepper to taste
12 cups (or more) chicken broth
1/4 cup (1 ounce) grated
Parmesan cheese

Sauté the onion in the olive oil in a large saucepan over medium-high heat until tender. Add the artichokes and season with salt and pepper. Cook for 10 minutes, stirring frequently. Add the broth. Reduce the heat and simmer for 20 minutes or until the artichokes are tender. Purée the mixture in batches in a food processor. Strain the mixture through a fine mesh strainer into the saucepan. Thin the soup with additional broth if necessary. Season to taste. Ladle into soup bowls and sprinkle with the Parmesan cheese.

Serves 8 to 10

Cuban Black Bean Soup

1 pound dried black beans, sorted
and rinsed
1 cup finely chopped cooked ham
1 cup chopped onion
1 large tomato, chopped
3 garlic cloves, minced
3 cups beef broth
1 3/4 cups water
1/4 cup dark rum or apple cider
2 tablespoons vegetable oil
1 1/2 teaspoons ground cumin
1 1/2 teaspoons dried oregano
Sour cream
Shredded Cheddar cheese

Combine the beans, ham, onion, tomato, garlic, broth, water, rum, oil, cumin and oregano in a 4- to 6-quart slow cooker and mix well. Cover and cook on High for 6 to 8 hours.

Serves 6

This is easy and good—destined to be a family favorite! Try garnishing it with sour cream and shredded Cheddar cheese.

White Chili

1 pound navy beans
6 cups (or more) chicken broth
2 garlic cloves, minced
2 onions, chopped
1 tablespoon vegetable oil
2 (4-ounce) cans mild green
   chiles, chopped
2 teaspoons ground cumin
1¹/2 teaspoons oregano
¹/4 teaspoon ground cloves
¹/4 teaspoon cayenne pepper
4 cups chopped cooked
   chicken breast
2 bay leaves (optional)
¹/4 teaspoon white pepper
1 teaspoon green Tabasco sauce
3 cups (12 ounces) shredded
   Monterey Jack cheese
   Salsa
   Sour cream

Combine the beans, broth, garlic and half the onions in a saucepan. Bring to a boil. Reduce the heat and simmer, covered, for 3 hours or until the beans are tender, adding more broth if necessary.

Sauté the remaining onion in the oil in a skillet until tender. Add the chiles, cumin, oregano, cloves and cayenne pepper and mix well. Stir into the bean mixture. Add the chicken and bay leaves and simmer for 1 hour. Remove and discard the bay leaves. Season with the white pepper and Tabasco sauce. Ladle into bowls and top with the cheese, salsa and sour cream.

Serves 8 to 10

The Spokane Veterans Memorial Arena

With a seating capacity of 12,500 and a fantastic scenic location near the river, the Spokane Arena opened in 1995 to "rave reviews." (See www.spokanearena.com.) The facility hosts an enormous variety of popular sporting events, such as Spokane Chiefs ice hockey and Eastern Washington University and Gonzaga University basketball. Music concerts are a big draw. The arena hosts musicians for every taste, from Lynyrd Skynyrd to Sting to Toby Keith. Spokanites are truly thrilled to be chosen as the host to the 2007 U.S. Figure Skating Championships. Visitors, competitors, and entertainers are sure to receive a warm Spokane welcome, and they are always welcomed back for more.

Cougar Gold, Apple and Onion Soup

5 cups chicken broth
1 cup chopped peeled potato
2 cooking apples, peeled, cored and chopped
1/2 cup chopped onion
1/4 cup chopped carrots
1/4 cup chopped celery
1/8 teaspoon ground thyme
2 tablespoons cornstarch
2 tablespoons cold water
4 cups (16 ounces) shredded Cougar Gold cheese
1/4 cup heavy cream or light cream
1/8 teaspoon nutmeg, preferably freshly ground
1/8 teaspoon white pepper
Salt to taste
1/4 cup dry white wine (optional)
Thin unpeeled apple slices

Combine the broth, potato, apples, onion, carrots, celery and thyme in a medium saucepan. Bring to a boil. Reduce the heat and simmer for 45 minutes or until the vegetables are tender. Purée the mixture in batches in a food processor.

Return the soup to the pan. Whisk the cornstarch and cold water in a small bowl until blended. Stir the mixture into the soup. Cook over medium heat until slightly thickened, stirring constantly. Add the cheese and cook until melted, stirring frequently. Add the cream, nutmeg and white pepper. Simmer for 5 minutes to blend the flavors, stirring constantly. Season with salt to taste. Stir in the wine just before serving. Top each serving with 3 slices of apple.

Serves 4 to 6

Cougar Gold cheese is a sharp white Cheddar made on the grounds of Washington State University in Pullman, Washington. The cheese is aged for a year and is delicious in soups or just sliced and served with whole wheat crackers.

Ultimate Comfort Chicken Noodle Soup

10 cups chicken broth
1 cup dry white wine (optional)
1 pound boneless skinless
   chicken breasts
1/4 cup (1/2 stick) unsalted butter
2 to 3 leeks, chopped (white
   parts only)
2 carrots, peeled and finely chopped
3 ribs celery, finely chopped
2 teaspoons salt
1 teaspoon pepper
2 cups drained cooked egg noodles
6 ounces frozen peas
3 tablespoons chopped fresh
   Italian parsley

Bring the broth and wine to a boil in a large saucepan. Reduce the heat and add the chicken. Simmer for 15 minutes or until the chicken is cooked through. Remove the chicken with a slotted spoon. Reserve the cooking liquid and let cool.

Melt the butter in a large heavy saucepan over low heat. Sauté the leeks, carrots, celery, salt and pepper for 5 minutes. Add the reserved cooking liquid and simmer for 10 minutes. Add the noodles and peas and simmer for 5 minutes. Remove from the heat. Shred the chicken and stir into the soup. Add the parsley and heat through, stirring frequently.

Serves 6 to 8

Hoopfest

In a city that is proud to be called home to the men's and women's award-winning Gonzaga basketball teams, as well as the strong basketball program of nearby Eastern Washington University, what could be more natural than a huge outdoor over-the-top basketball tournament? That is Hoopfest! Proudly described on its Web site as "the biggest 3-on-3 street basketball tournament on the planet" (www.hoopfest.org), every summer it draws more than six thousand teams of every imaginable age and ability to downtown Spokane. Hoopfesters take up more than four hundred basketball courts spanning forty downtown city blocks.

In keeping with other Spokane civic events, it isn't all about fun! With a committee emphasis on Special Olympics and building city-wide outdoor basketball courts, the Hoopfest organization is responsible for more than $700,000 in donations to numerous charitable organizations.

Spicy Lentil Soup

1¼ cups dried red lentils
2½ cups water
 2 chicken bouillon cubes
 2 garlic cloves, minced
 1 cup chopped carrots
 1 cup chopped celery
 8 ounces spicy sausage, cooked
   and chopped
 2 tablespoons red wine or red
   wine vinegar
 1 tablespoon minced fresh thyme
 1 tablespoon olive oil
 1 teaspoon salt
 ½ teaspoon pepper

Rinse the lentils several times; drain. Bring the water and bouillon cubes to a boil in a saucepan. Add the lentils, garlic, carrots and celery and mix well. Reduce the heat and add the sausage. Simmer, covered, for 20 to 30 minutes or until the lentils are tender and most of the liquid has been absorbed. Stir in the wine, thyme, olive oil, salt and pepper.

Note: Lentils should not be cooked in aluminum or cast-iron pans because they can prevent cooking and alter the color.

Serves 4

The first lentils grown in the United States were grown in the Palouse region of Washington, just outside of Spokane. The region's weather and nutrient-rich volcanic soils are a great combination for lentils, dry peas, and chick-peas.

THE PEA & LENTIL COOKBOOK, *USA Dry Pea & Lentil Council*

Chilled Alderwood-Smoked Salmon Bisque

 3 tablespoons unsalted butter
 ⅓ cup finely chopped shallots
 1 (8-ounce) piece of alderwood-
   smoked salmon
 6 ounces cream cheese, softened
1½ cups heavy cream
 1 cup milk
 ½ cup plus 2 tablespoons
   sour cream
   Sprigs of dill weed

Melt the butter in a medium saucepan over low heat. Sauté the shallots in the butter until tender. Add the salmon and cook for 1 minute. Add the cream cheese. Cook until the cream cheese is melted, stirring constantly. Purée the mixture in a blender or food processor until smooth. Combine the cream, milk and sour cream in a bowl and mix well. Add to the salmon mixture and process until smooth. Chill, covered, in the refrigerator for several hours. Garnish with fresh dill weed and serve with dark wheat bread.

Serves 4

Pea and Pesto Soup

THE PEA & LENTIL COOKBOOK, *USA Dry Pea & Lentil Council*

1 cup dried green peas or yellow
  split peas, rinsed
1 (14-ounce) can chicken broth
2¹/₂ cups water
3 tablespoons basil pesto
1 cup thinly sliced zucchini
1 cup chopped green onions
  Croutons
  Grated Parmesan cheese

Bring the peas, broth and water to a boil in a large saucepan over high heat. Simmer, covered, for 35 to 45 minutes or until the peas are tender. Stir in the pesto, zucchini and green onions. Simmer for 5 to 10 minutes longer. Ladle into bowls and top with croutons and cheese.

Note: Try making this with our Jan's Perfect Pesto recipe on page 111.

Serves 4

Northwest Wild Mushroom Soup

6 tablespoons butter
1 pound assorted wild
  mushrooms, chopped
1 pound chanterelle
  mushrooms, chopped
  Juice of 1 lemon
1 bay leaf
¹/₂ teaspoon thyme
2 tablespoons minced shallots
4 cups heavy cream
3 cups chicken broth
2 teaspoons salt
1 teaspoon pepper
1 cup cooked wild rice
2 teaspoons cornstarch mixed with
  2 tablespoons water
¹/₂ cup minced fresh parsley
  (optional)

Melt the butter in a large saucepan. Add the mushrooms, lemon juice, bay leaf, thyme and shallots. Cook, covered, over medium-low heat for 15 to 20 minutes. Add the cream, broth, salt, pepper and wild rice and mix well. Bring to a boil. Reduce the heat and simmer for 20 to 30 minutes. Stir in the cornstarch mixture. Simmer for 10 to 15 minutes longer, stirring frequently. Remove and discard the bay leaf. Ladle into bowls and sprinkle each serving with the parsley.

Note: Chanterelles are trumpet-shaped wild mushrooms that are native to the Northwest.

Serves 6

Warming Winter Squash Soup

2 (2-pound) acorn squash
1 (2-pound) buttercup squash
1 (2-pound) butternut squash
1 small spaghetti squash
   Salt and white pepper to taste
10 tablespoons butter
10 teaspoons molasses
2 carrots, peeled, halved lengthwise
1 leek, trimmed and chopped
1 onion, finely chopped
6 garlic cloves
2 cups white wine
8 cups chicken broth
1 teaspoon allspice
1/4 teaspoon nutmeg
1/2 cup heavy cream
2 tablespoons butter
1 tablespoon finely
   chopped parsley
2 tablespoons sour cream
1 tablespoon chopped chives

Preheat the oven to 350 degrees. Cut the squash into halves lengthwise and scoop out the seeds. Season with salt and white pepper. Arrange the halves skin side down in a shallow roasting pan. Place 1 tablespoon butter and 1 teaspoon molasses in the center of each half. Arrange the carrots, leek, onion and garlic cloves around the squash. Pour 1 cup of the wine and 1 cup of the broth into the pan. Cover with foil and bake for 2 hours.

Remove from the oven and cool for 5 minutes. Scoop the flesh of the acorn squash, buttercup squash and butternut squash into a large saucepan, discarding the skins. Scoop the spaghetti squash flesh into a bowl and set aside. Add the roasted vegetables and the cooking liquid. Add the remaining 1 cup wine and 7 cups broth to the pan. Bring to a boil; reduce to a simmer. Add the allspice, nutmeg, salt and white pepper. Simmer for 10 minutes, stirring occasionally. Remove from the heat. Purée with an immersion blender until smooth. Stir in the cream and season with salt and white pepper. Melt 2 tablespoons butter in a large skillet. Sauté the reserved spaghetti squash in the butter for 2 minutes. Stir in the parsley. Ladle the soup into shallow bowls. Top with the spaghetti squash mixture, sour cream and chives.

Serves 8 to 10

Sausage Tortellini Soup

1¹/₂ pounds Italian sausage
2 tablespoons olive oil
2 cups sliced zucchini
1 cup chopped green bell pepper
1 yellow onion, chopped
2 large garlic cloves, chopped
1¹/₂ teaspoons oregano leaves
4 (14-ounce) cans chicken broth
1 (8-ounce) can tomatoes
12 ounces tri-color cheese tortellini
1 (6-ounce) can sliced black olives
    Grated Parmesan cheese
    Garlic bread toasts

Remove the sausage casings and brown the sausage in the olive oil in a large saucepan, breaking up any clumps with a wooden spoon. Add the zucchini, bell pepper, onion, garlic, oregano, broth and tomatoes. Bring to a boil and reduce the heat. Simmer for 10 minutes, stirring frequently. Return to a boil and add the tortellini and olives. Simmer for 15 to 20 minutes or until the tortellini are tender. Ladle into bowls and garnish with cheese and garlic bread toasts.

Serves 6 to 8

Pumpkin Soup

¹/₄ cup (¹/₂ stick) butter
6 green onions, chopped
1 medium to large onion, sliced
3 cups pumpkin purée
6 cups chicken broth
¹/₂ teaspoon salt
3 tablespoons all-purpose flour
2 tablespoons butter
    White pepper to taste
1 cup half-and-half
1 tablespoon butter
2 tablespoons lime juice, or to taste
    Finely chopped parsley
    Crème fraîche
    Shelled pumpkin seeds (pepitas)

Melt ¹/₄ cup butter in a large saucepan. Add the onions. Sauté until the onions are golden brown and tender. Add the pumpkin purée, broth and salt. Bring to a boil. Reduce the heat and simmer for 10 minutes, stirring occasionally. Strain the soup, discarding the solids. You may refrigerate the soup at this point. Return the soup to the saucepan and heat through.

Knead the flour and 2 tablespoons butter together. Add to the soup gradually, whisking constantly. Bring to a boil. Boil until thickened, whisking constantly. Season with white pepper. Stir in the half-and-half, 1 tablespoon butter and the lime juice. Cook until heated through. Ladle into soup bowls. Garnish the soup with parsley, crème fraîche and pumpkin seeds. (Toast the pumpkin seeds lightly for the best flavor.)

Serves 8

"Don't Kiss Me in the Morning" Caesar Salad

1 small egg yolk
3 large garlic cloves
8 anchovy fillets, finely chopped
1 teaspoon Dijon mustard
  Juice of 1/2 lemon
2 dashes of Tabasco sauce
1 teaspoon Worcestershire sauce
1 teaspoon red wine vinegar
1/4 cup olive oil
1/2 cup (2 ounces) grated
  Parmesan cheese
  Salt and pepper to taste
1 head romaine
1 cup garlic croutons

Whisk the egg yolk with the garlic and anchovies in a small bowl. Whisk in the mustard, lemon juice, Tabasco sauce, Worcestershire sauce, vinegar, olive oil, cheese, salt and pepper.

Tear the lettuce into bite-size pieces and place in a large salad bowl. Pour the dressing over the lettuce and toss to combine. Top with the croutons.

Serves 4

Not just your average Caesar!

Corn Salad with Cilantro Jalapeño Dressing

Cilantro Jalapeño Dressing

1 1/2 cups chopped cilantro
3/4 cup extra-virgin olive oil
1/3 cup white wine vinegar
3 tablespoons lemon juice
2 jalapeño chiles, chopped
1 teaspoon ground ginger

Corn Salad

1 (32-ounce) package frozen corn
1 small onion, diced
1 1/2 tablespoons vegetable oil
1 red bell pepper, diced
1 green bell pepper, diced

For the dressing, combine the cilantro, olive oil, vinegar, lemon juice, jalapeño chiles and ginger in a blender and process until smooth.

For the salad, thaw the corn. Sauté the onion in the oil in a skillet over medium heat for 3 minutes. Add the bell peppers and cook for 2 minutes longer. Combine the corn, onion and bell peppers in a bowl and mix well. Pour the dressing over the salad and toss to combine. Chill in the refrigerator.

Note: To reduce the heat in a jalapeño chile, cut out the seeds and ribs and rinse the inside of the chile.

Serves 4 to 6

Curried Chicken Salad Lettuce Wraps

1 cup mayonnaise
1/4 to 1/3 cup mango chutney
1 1/2 teaspoons curry powder
2 tablespoons heavy cream or
sour cream
Juice of 1/2 lime
2 cups chopped cooked
chicken breast
1 cup chopped celery
1 cup grape halves
1 cup coarsely chopped walnuts
or pecans
1 cup shredded coconut
Iceberg lettuce leaves, chilled

Combine the mayonnaise, chutney, curry powder, cream and lime juice in a medium bowl and mix well. Chill, covered, in the refrigerator. Combine the chicken, celery, grapes, walnuts and coconut in a large bowl and mix well. Add enough of the mayonnaise mixture to moisten the salad and mix well. The salad mixture can be prepared in advance, omitting the coconut. Add it at serving time.

Place 1/4 to 1/2 cup of the salad mixture in the center of each lettuce leaf. Wrap the sides of the lettuce around the filling to enclose. Use any leftover dressing as a dipping sauce.

Note: Mango chutney is a traditional Indian condiment available in most grocery stores.

Serves 4 to 6

Davenport Hotel's Crab Louis

3/4 cup mayonnaise
1/4 cup chili sauce
1 1/2 tablespoons lemon juice
2 tablespoons heavy cream
2 tablespoons sliced green onions
2 heads butter lettuce
4 hard-cooked eggs, sliced
12 tomato wedges
1 pound fresh Dungeness
crab meat, drained and flaked
1/2 cup diced red and yellow
bell pepper
Lemon wedges

Combine the mayonnaise, chili sauce, lemon juice, cream and green onions in a blender and process until smooth or combine all ingredients in a bowl and mix well.

Cut the lettuce heads into halves. Arrange 1/2 head on each of four plates. Top with the eggs and tomato wedges. Spoon 4 ounces crab meat into the center of the lettuce. Sprinkle with bell pepper and drizzle with the dressing. Garnish each plate with a lemon wedge.

Note: This salad tastes best when made with the freshest crab meat possible.

Serves 4

Autumn in Spokane Salad

Curried Cashews

- 3 ounces cashew halves
- 1 tablespoon butter, melted
- 1 teaspoon fresh rosemary
- 1 teaspoon curry powder
- 1 teaspoon dark brown sugar
- 1/2 teaspoon sea salt
- 1/8 teaspoon cayenne pepper

Garlic Honey Dressing

- 3 tablespoons white wine vinegar
- 3 tablespoons Dijon mustard
- 2 tablespoons honey
- 1 teaspoon minced garlic
  Salt and pepper to taste
- 1/2 cup vegetable oil

Salad

- 8 ounces bacon, crisp-cooked and crumbled
- 12 cups loosely packed spinach
- 6 cups chopped hearts of romaine
- 2/3 cup thinly sliced shallots
- 3 small pears, halved, cored and thinly sliced

For the curried cashews, toast the cashews in a 400-degree oven until golden brown. Let cool slightly. Combine with the butter, rosemary, curry powder, brown sugar, salt and cayenne pepper in a bowl and stir to coat.

For the dressing, combine the vinegar, mustard, honey, garlic, salt and pepper in a bowl and whisk to blend. Whisk in the oil gradually.

For the salad, combine the bacon, spinach, romaine, shallots and pears in a large bowl and mix well.

To serve, top the salad with the cashews and toss with the dressing.

Serves 6 to 8

Greenbluff

Where can you go to find tree-ripened apples, luscious peaches, and the sweetest strawberries, all just waiting to be picked? Greenbluff, that's where! Nestled in the green hills below Mt. Spokane, Greenbluff has bountiful orchards with a huge variety of delicious fruit, from the classic crisp Washington apple (every variety imaginable) to cherries, apricots, and berries. Vegetables such as pumpkins and sugar carrots attract fans from all over.

(continued on page 73)

Summery Asian Vermicelli

Soy Ginger Dressing

- 1/4 cup vegetable oil
- 3 tablespoons rice vinegar
- 3 tablespoons low-sodium soy sauce
- 2 teaspoons sugar
- 1/8 teaspoon cayenne pepper
- 1 teaspoon finely chopped fresh gingerroot
- 1 garlic clove, minced

Salad

- 8 ounces thin spaghetti
- 3/4 cup julienned carrots
- 3/4 cup julienned zucchini
- 3/4 cup chopped red bell pepper
- 1/3 cup sliced green onions
- 12 ounces cooked chicken breasts, chopped
  Chopped cilantro
  Toasted cashews

For the dressing, combine the oil, vinegar, soy sauce, sugar, cayenne pepper, gingerroot and garlic in a bowl or a jar with a tight-fitting lid. Whisk or shake to combine.

For the salad, cook the spaghetti using the package directions; drain and let cool. Combine the spaghetti with the carrots, zucchini, bell pepper, green onions and chicken in a large bowl and mix well. Add the dressing, tossing to coat. Top with the cilantro and cashews. Chill, covered, in the refrigerator for 2 hours or longer.

Serves 6

There is something going on in Greenbluff just about all year long. June finds countless children with their families, happily filling themselves up on strawberries while their parents pick away. As cherries ripen in July, there is the famous "Cherry Pickers' Trot and Pit Spit." Visitors compete to see who can spit their cherry pit the farthest. If that is not enough, there is also a four-mile run through the orchards. By August, it is Peach Festival time! Lucky pickers sample huge peaches dripping with sweet juice. September just would not be complete without a visit to Greenbluff to pick apples, run through a corn maze, and select the perfect pumpkin. By December, there are lovely Christmas trees waiting to be cut as tree seekers enjoy hot chocolate, sleigh rides, and holiday celebrations in the snow.

Mediterranean Pasta Salad

Basil Vinaigrette

$2/3$ cup olive oil

2 tablespoons chopped fresh basil

3 tablespoons red wine vinegar

2 tablespoons chopped
green onions

2 tablespoons grated
Parmesan cheese

$1^1/4$ teaspoons salt

$1/4$ teaspoon pepper

Pasta Salad

12 ounces pasta, cooked
and drained

1 small red bell pepper, diced

1 small red bell pepper, diced

1 small yellow bell pepper, diced

1 tomato, chopped

$1/4$ cup toasted pine nuts

$1/4$ cup black olives, sliced

6 tablespoons chopped fresh basil

8 ounces mozzarella cheese, cubed

1 tablespoon dried basil

$1/4$ teaspoon crumbled dried oregano

For the vinaigrette, combine the olive oil, basil, vinegar, green onions, cheese, salt and pepper in a blender or food processor. Process until well combined.

For the salad, combine the pasta, bell peppers, tomato, pine nuts, olives and 6 tablespoons basil in a large bowl and mix well. Pour the vinaigrette over the salad and stir gently to combine.

Roll the cheese cubes in the dried basil and add to the salad. Sprinkle with the oregano and mix well. Serve at room temperature.

Serves 8 to 10

Toast the pine nuts in a skillet over medium-low heat until brown and fragrant, watching carefully and shaking the skillet frequently.

Northwest Spinach Salad with Apple and Cheddar

Maple Dressing
- 1/3 cup each balsamic vinegar, maple syrup and olive oil
  Salt and pepper to taste

Salad
- 1 pound baby spinach
- 2 Granny Smith apples, halved, cored and thinly sliced
- 8 ounces extra-sharp Cheddar cheese, cut into 1/2-inch cubes
- 1/2 cup chopped toasted walnuts

For the dressing, combine the vinegar, maple syrup and olive oil in a bowl or a jar with a tight-fitting lid. Whisk or shake to blend. Season with salt and pepper to taste.

For the salad, combine the spinach, apples, cheese and walnuts in a large bowl and mix well. Pour the dressing over the salad and toss to coat.

Serves 6

A great salad for fall!

Spokane Blue Spinach Salad

Blueberry Vinaigrette
- 1 shallot, minced
- 1/2 pint fresh blueberries
- 1 teaspoon salt
- 3 tablespoons sugar
- 1/3 cup raspberry vinegar
- 1 cup vegetable oil

Salad
- 2 bunches spinach, stemmed, washed and dried
- 1 pint fresh blueberries
- 2/3 cup crumbled blue cheese
- 1/2 cup chopped toasted pecans

For the dressing, combine the shallot, blueberries, salt, sugar, vinegar and oil in a blender. Process until well mixed.

For the salad, combine the spinach, blueberries, cheese and pecans in a large bowl and mix well. Top the salad with vinaigrette to taste and toss to coat. Store leftover vinaigrette in the refrigerator for up to 2 months.

Note: Spinach grows best in sandy, gritty soil, so it is a good idea to wash even "pre-washed" spinach thoroughly. Also, be sure to remove any tough stems. When buying spinach, look for bright green color, with no yellowing.

Serves 4

Try this salad at a summer party, when blueberries are in season. Guests will insist on getting the recipe.

Greenbluff Strawberry Spinach Salad

Citrus Poppy Seed Dressing

- 1 orange
- 2 tablespoons white wine vinegar
- 1/3 cup sugar
- 1 tablespoon vegetable oil
- 1 teaspoon poppy seeds

Salad

- 8 ounces (1 1/2 cups) strawberries
- 1/2 cucumber
- 6 ounces baby spinach
- 1/4 cup chopped shallots
- 1/2 cup feta cheese
- 1/4 cup sliced almonds, toasted

For the dressing, zest the orange and measure out 1/2 teaspoon. Juice the orange into a bowl and measure out 2 tablespoons. Combine 1/2 teaspoon orange zest, 2 tablespoons orange juice, the vinegar, sugar, oil and poppy seeds in a bowl or a jar with a tight-fitting lid. Whisk or shake to combine.

For the salad, hull the strawberries and cut into quarters. Cut the cucumber into halves lengthwise and slice. Combine the spinach, strawberries, cucumber, shallots and cheese in a large bowl. Pour the dressing over the salad, tossing to coat. Sprinkle with the almonds.

Serves 8 to 10

Zesty Spinach Salad

- 1 cup vegetable oil
- 1/2 cup sugar
- 1/4 cup red wine vinegar
- 1/3 cup ketchup
- 2 tablespoons Worcestershire sauce
- 1/2 teaspoon salt
- 3 green onions, sliced
- 8 ounces bacon
- 10 ounces fresh spinach
- 8 ounces fresh bean sprouts
- 1 (8-ounce) can sliced water chestnuts
- 4 hard-cooked eggs, sliced

Combine the oil, sugar, vinegar, ketchup, Worcestershire sauce and salt in a blender. Process until smooth. Add the green onions and process briefly.

Cook the bacon until crisp; drain and crumble. Rinse and drain the spinach and bean sprouts. Combine in a large bowl. Drain the water chestnuts and add to the salad. Add the bacon and toss with the salad. Top with the eggs. Add the dressing and toss to coat.

Serves 6

Super Slaw with Peanut Dressing

Peanut Dressing

    6 tablespoons rice vinegar
    6 tablespoons canola oil
    5 tablespoons creamy peanut butter
1 1/2 tablespoons minced garlic
    3 tablespoons soy sauce
    3 tablespoons brown sugar
    2 tablespoons minced fresh
       gingerroot

Slaw

    5 cups thinly sliced green cabbage
    2 cups thinly sliced red cabbage
    2 large red or yellow bell peppers,
       cut into matchsticks
    8 large green onions, sliced
  3/4 cup chopped cilantro
       Salt and pepper to taste

For the dressing, whisk the vinegar, canola oil, peanut butter, garlic, soy sauce, sugar and gingerroot in a bowl until well blended. (The dressing can be made a day ahead and stored in the refrigerator.)

For the slaw, combine the cabbages, bell peppers, green onions and cilantro in a large bowl and mix well. Add the dressing and toss to coat. Season with salt and pepper to taste.

Serves 8 to 10

The peanutty flavor of this unusual slaw is a delicious surprise. Great with grilled meats!

Wonderful Watermelon Salad

    1 small watermelon, seeded and
       cut into chunks
    1 pint blueberries
  1/3 cup finely chopped fresh mint
    6 ounces feta cheese, crumbled

Combine the watermelon, blueberries and mint in a bowl and mix well. Chill, covered, in the refrigerator for a few hours. Drain before serving. Top with the cheese.

Serves 8 to 10

A great salad for a Fourth of July barbecue!

Topper's Greek Salad

Dill Chive Dressing

- 1 tablespoon chives
- 5 tablespoons olive oil
- 1 tablespoon fresh dill weed
- 2 tablespoons balsamic vinegar
- 1 teaspoon sugar
  Salt and pepper to taste

Salad

- 8 ounces zucchini
- 1 small red onion, thinly sliced
- 4 small tomatoes, cut into wedges
- 1 green bell pepper, cut into strips
  Kalamata olives, sliced
- 1 (6-ounce) jar green olives
- 2 hard-cooked eggs, sliced
- 8 ounces feta cheese

For the dressing, combine the chives, olive oil, dill weed, vinegar, sugar, salt and pepper in a bowl or a jar with a tight-fitting lid. Whisk or shake to blend.

For the salad, slice the zucchini into rounds. Combine the zucchini, onion, tomatoes and bell pepper in a bowl or on a salad platter. Drain the olives and arrange over the vegetables. Top with the eggs. Pour the dressing over the salad and crumble the cheese over the top.

Serves 4 to 6

Huckleberry Poppy Seed Dressing

- 1 pasteurized egg, or equivalent amount of egg substitute
- 2 tablespoons huckleberry syrup
- 1 tablespoon Dijon mustard
- 2/3 cup huckleberry vinegar
- 1/2 teaspoon salt
- 3 tablespoons grated yellow onion
- 2 cups canola oil
- 3 tablespoons poppy seeds

Combine the egg, syrup, mustard, vinegar, salt and onion in a blender or food processor. Process until well combined. Add the canola oil in a fine stream, processing constantly until blended. Pour the mixture into a bowl. Stir in the poppy seeds. Chill, covered, in the refrigerator.

Toss with fruit for an easy fruit salad!

Makes about 3 cups dressing

Washington Apple, Potato, Onion Gratin

1/4 cup (1/2 stick) butter
2 pounds Walla Walla sweet
  onions, sliced
2 tablespoons chopped fresh thyme
2 teaspoons salt
1/4 cup (1/2 stick) butter,
  cut into pieces
1/3 cup water
1 cup dry white wine
2 teaspoons sugar
2 1/2 pounds Yukon gold potatoes,
  thinly sliced
2 pounds tart apples, such as
  Granny Smith, peeled, cored,
  halved and thinly sliced
2 teaspoons salt

Preheat the oven to 400 degrees. Melt 1/4 cup butter in a large skillet over medium heat. Add the onions, thyme and 2 teaspoons salt. Sauté the mixture for 8 minutes or until the onions are tender and begin to color. Remove from the heat and add 1/4 cup butter, the water, wine and sugar to the skillet. Return to the heat, stirring and swirling the skillet to combine. Bring to a boil. Remove from the heat and cool to lukewarm. Combine the potatoes, apples, 2 teaspoons salt and the onion mixture in a large bowl and toss gently to combine. Spoon into a greased 9×13-inch baking dish. Bake, covered, for 55 minutes or until the potatoes are tender. Bake, uncovered, for 20 minutes or until the top is brown and bubbly.

Serves 10 to 12

Sweet and Spicy Carrots

3 carrots, or 3 cups baby carrots
1 cup water
1 small onion, minced
1/2 cup mayonnaise
1 to 2 tablespoons horseradish
1/2 teaspoon salt
1/4 teaspoon pepper
1 slice bread
1 tablespoon butter, softened
1 teaspoon chopped parsley

Preheat the oven to 375 degrees. Julienne the carrots. Cook the carrots in the water in a large saucepan over medium heat until tender. Drain, reserving 1/4 cup liquid. Place the carrots in a buttered shallow 1 1/2-quart baking dish. Mix the reserved cooking liquid, onion, mayonnaise, horseradish, salt and pepper in a bowl. Spoon over the carrots. Spread the bread with the butter. Place in a food processor and process until crumbly. Sprinkle over the carrot mixture. Bake for 15 to 20 minutes. Sprinkle with the parsley.

Serves 4

Spicy Corn on the Cob

4 ears of corn
Salt to taste
1/4 cup vegetable oil
1/3 cup freshly grated
   Parmesan cheese
2 garlic cloves, minced
2 tablespoons fresh lime juice
1 teaspoon ground cumin
1/2 teaspoon hot red pepper sauce
1/3 cup chopped fresh cilantro

Cook the corn in boiling salted water in a saucepan for 5 minutes or until tender; drain. Set aside 1 tablespoon of the oil. Combine the remaining oil, the cheese, garlic, lime juice, cumin and hot pepper sauce in a bowl and mix well. Sauté the corn in the reserved oil in a skillet for about 2 minutes. Brush with the cheese mixture and continue to cook until the corn begins to brown. Add the cilantro to the cheese mixture and brush over the corn. Serve immediately.

Serves 4

For a different twist, try grilling the corn. Just omit the Parmesan cheese and turn the corn about four times to cook all sides.

Norwegian Cucumbers

1 seedless English cucumber
1/2 cup white vinegar
2 tablespoons water
2 tablespoons sugar
   Salt and pepper to taste
1/4 cup finely chopped fresh
   dill weed
1 red onion, thinly sliced

Score the cucumber with a fork and cut into thin slices. Combine the cucumber with the vinegar, water, sugar, salt, pepper, dill weed and onion in a large bowl and mix well. Chill in the refrigerator for 3 hours to allow the flavors to blend.

Serves 6

Italian Green Beans

1 garlic clove, minced
1/4 cup olive oil
1 (14-ounce) can stewed tomatoes, preferably Italian-style
1 teaspoon chopped fresh oregano
1 teaspoon chopped fresh basil
1 teaspoon garlic salt (optional)
1 pound fresh or frozen whole green beans, trimmed
Salt and pepper to taste

Sauté the garlic in the olive oil in a large skillet for 1 to 2 minutes. Add the tomatoes, breaking up any large pieces. Add the oregano, basil and garlic salt and mix well. Bring to a boil and reduce the heat. Simmer for 10 minutes, stirring frequently. Add the green beans. Cook for 20 minutes, stirring occasionally. Season with salt and pepper to taste. Serve hot.

Serves 4

Green Beans with Potatoes and Tomatoes

1 1/2 pounds green beans, trimmed
2 pounds small red new potatoes, quartered
2 tablespoons orange juice
2 tablespoons white wine vinegar
1 pint cherry tomatoes, cut into halves
2 tablespoons chopped fresh Italian parsley
6 tablespoons orange juice
1 tablespoon white wine vinegar
1/3 cup extra-virgin olive oil
6 tablespoons drained capers
Salt and pepper to taste

Cook the beans in a large pot of boiling salted water for 4 minutes or until tender-crisp. Plunge into ice water to stop the cooking; drain.

Cook the potatoes in a large pot with water to cover over medium-high heat for 8 minutes or until tender; drain. Combine the potatoes with 2 tablespoons orange juice and 2 tablespoons vinegar in a large bowl. Toss to coat. Let cool to room temperature.

Add the green beans, tomatoes and parsley to the potato mixture and mix well. Whisk 6 tablespoons orange juice, 1 tablespoon vinegar, the olive oil and capers in a small bowl until combined. Season with salt and pepper to taste. Pour the mixture over the vegetables and toss to coat. Serve at room temperature.

Serves 10 to 12

A colorful dish that is great for a cookout!

Easy Sweet Onions

1 very large Walla Walla
  sweet onion
1 beef bouillon cube
1/2 teaspoon brown sugar
1/4 cup water

Cut a hole the center of the onion about the size of a ping-pong ball. Place the bouillon cube, brown sugar and water in the hole. Place the onion in a small bowl and cover with plastic wrap. Microwave for 6 to 7 minutes or until tender and cooked through. (Or wrap in foil and grill until tender.)

Serves 1

Walla Walla sweet onions are typically in season from the middle of June through September.

Sweet Onion Rings

1/2 cup milk
1/2 cup beer
1/4 cup vegetable oil
2 egg yolks
1 teaspoon salt
  Freshly ground pepper to taste
1 1/4 cups all-purpose flour
3 large Vidalia onions, sliced and
  separated into rings
4 cups milk
3 egg whites
  Vegetable oil for deep-frying

Whisk 1/2 cup milk, the beer, 1/4 cup oil, the egg yolks, salt and pepper in a large bowl until blended. Sift in the flour and mix well. Chill, covered, in the refrigerator for 1 1/2 hours. Let stand at room temperature for 30 minutes. Place the onion rings in a large shallow dish and cover with 4 cups milk. Soak the onions in the milk for 30 minutes or until soft. Beat the egg whites in a mixing bowl until soft peaks form; fold them into the beer batter. Preheat the oven to 200 degrees.

Fill a wok or deep-sided skillet one-third full with oil and heat to 375 degrees. Dip the onion rings into the batter a few at a time. Lift the rings out individually using tongs, shaking off any extra batter. Drop the onion rings gently into the hot oil. Fry for 2 to 3 minutes per side or until golden brown. Drain on a paper towel-lined baking sheet. Keep the onion rings warm in the oven for 3 to 4 minutes or until ready to serve.

Serves 6

Mashed Potatoes and Parsnips

6 pounds russet potatoes, peeled
   and cut into 1¹/₂-inch pieces
   Salt to taste
1 cup (or more) buttermilk
¹/₂ cup (1 stick) butter, softened
   Freshly ground pepper to taste
4 pounds parsnips, cut into
   ¹/₂-inch pieces
¹/₄ cup (¹/₂ stick) butter, softened
2 teaspoons fresh lemon juice
   Chopped fresh parsley

Cook the potatoes in a large pot of boiling salted water for 25 minutes or until very tender. Drain well; return to the pot. Cook over medium heat for about 3 minutes or until any excess liquid evaporates, stirring constantly. Add 1 cup buttermilk and ¹/₂ cup butter. Mash the potatoes until almost smooth, thinning with additional buttermilk if needed. Season with salt and pepper to taste.

Cook the parsnips in a large pot of boiling salted water for 20 minutes or until very tender. Drain; return to the pot. Add ¹/₄ cup butter and the lemon juice. Mash until smooth. Season with salt and pepper to taste.

Spoon the potatoes into a large shallow bowl and make a well in the center. Spoon the parsnips into the well. Sprinkle with parsley.

Serves 12

Wonderful comfort food!

Red Potato Skewers with Dijon Mustard

2 pounds small red new potatoes,
   washed and cut into halves
   Salt to taste
¹/₄ cup olive oil
¹/₄ cup Dijon mustard
4 garlic cloves, minced
2 tablespoons finely chopped
   fresh rosemary
   Pepper to taste

Soak ten bamboo skewers in water for 30 minutes. Cook the potatoes in a large pot of boiling salted water for 10 minutes or until tender; drain. Preheat the broiler. Whisk the olive oil, mustard, garlic, rosemary, salt and pepper in a large bowl until blended. Add the potatoes to the dressing and toss to coat. Thread the potatoes onto the skewers. Arrange the potato skewers on a foil-lined baking sheet. Broil cut side up for about 5 minutes or until brown and sizzling, turning occasionally.

Makes 10 skewers

Sweet Potato Fries

1 teaspoon sea salt or kosher salt
2 teaspoons paprika
1 teaspoon coarsely ground
   black pepper
1/2 teaspoon garlic powder
1/2 teaspoon onion powder
1/2 teaspoon chili powder
4 sweet potatoes, peeled and cut
   into "steak fries"
2 teaspoons olive oil

Preheat the oven to 450 degrees. Combine the salt, paprika, pepper, garlic powder, onion powder and chili powder in a bowl and mix well. Combine the sweet potatoes and olive oil in a large sealable plastic bag. Seal the bag and toss to coat. Sprinkle the sweet potatoes with the spice mixture and toss again. Spread in a roasting pan or over a baking sheet and bake for 30 minutes.

Serves 4

Great Grilled Vegetables

Marinade
1 cup olive oil
1/3 cup balsamic vinegar
1/4 cup sherry
3 garlic cloves, minced
1 tablespoon Italian seasoning
2 teaspoons salt
1 teaspoon pepper

Vegetables
Zucchini, quartered lengthwise and cut into halves or thirds
Sweet onions, cut into chunks
Red or other bell peppers, cut into 2-inch pieces
Mushrooms, cut into halves

For the marinade, whisk the olive oil, vinegar, sherry, garlic, Italian seasoning, salt and pepper in a bowl until blended. (The mixture will keep in the refrigerator for several weeks.)

For the vegetables, place the zucchini, onions, bell peppers and mushrooms in a sealable plastic bag. Add enough marinade to generously coat the vegetables. Seal the bag and toss to coat. Marinate for 1 hour or longer. Remove from the marinade, discarding the marinade. Grill over hot coals until the vegetables are tender.

Variable servings

Coconut and Lime Rice

2³/4 cups chicken broth
2 cups long grain rice
¹/2 cup dried unsweetened
shredded coconut
¹/3 cup fresh mint, chopped
2 tablespoons cilantro, chopped
Grated zest and juice of 1 lime

Preheat the oven to 350 degrees. Place the broth and rice in a large saucepan. Bring to a boil over medium-high heat. Stir, cover and reduce the heat to low. Simmer for 15 to 20 minutes or until the liquid has been absorbed. Spread the coconut on a baking sheet. Bake for 7 to 10 minutes or until golden brown. Remove the rice from the heat and let stand, covered, for 5 minutes. Stir in the coconut, mint, cilantro, lime zest and lime juice and mix well. Serve warm.

Serves 6 to 8

Barley Nut Pilaf

1 cup pearl barley
6 tablespoons butter
¹/2 cup chopped pecans
1 cup chopped sweet onion,
such as Walla Walla sweets
8 ounces sliced mushrooms
¹/2 cup chopped fresh parsley
¹/4 teaspoon salt
¹/4 teaspoon pepper
3¹/3 cups chicken broth

Preheat the oven to 350 degrees. Rinse the barley in cold water; drain. Heat the butter in a 10-inch skillet over medium heat. Add the pecans. Cook until golden brown and fragrant, stirring frequently. Remove with a slotted spoon and set aside. Sauté the onion and barley until the barley is toasted. Remove from the heat. Stir in the pecans, parsley, salt and pepper. Spoon into a 2-quart baking dish. Bring the broth to a boil in a saucepan. Pour the broth over the barley mixture, stirring to combine. Bake for 1 hour and 10 minutes.

Serves 4 to 6

According to the Walla Walla Sweet Onion Growers Association, there are approximately forty growers cultivating sweet onions on about 1,200 acres. The onions are prized for their unique mellow flavor. Brought to the Pacific Northwest as a seed by a French soldier more than a century ago, the onions have been highly sought after ever since.

Main Events

MEATS & POULTRY

Grilled Prime Rib of Beef with
Garlic and Rosemary
88

PJ's Prime Rib Roast
89

Sizzling Summer Sirloins
89

Beef Tenderloin with
Cranberries
90

Lime-Grilled Flank Steak
90

Chili-Rubbed Flank Steak
91

3R Party Brisket
91

Tacos al Carbon
92

Slow-Cooker French Dip
92

Marvelous Muffalettas
93

Pork Tenderloin Medallions
with Port and
Bing Cherry Sauce
94

RJ's Barbecue Sauce
94

Pork Tenderloin with
Herbed Crumb Crust
95

Asian Grilled Pork Tenderloins
95

Dry-Rubbed Baby Back Ribs
with Molasses Barbecue Sauce
96

Curried Pork and
Onion Skewers with
Mango Pineapple Salsa
97

Pork Chops with
Northwest Mushrooms
98

Apricot-Glazed Pork Chops
99

Black Rock Elk Chops in
Huckleberry Port Reduction
100

Camp Jack Lamb Stew,
Moroccan Style
101

Chicken with Bacon,
Mushrooms and Spinach
102

Chicken Kiev
103

Honey Lime Chicken
103

Ginger-Marinated Chicken
104

Crispy Pub Mustard Chicken
104

Chicken Joseph
105

Chicken Breasts with
Prosciutto and Sage
106

Bourbon Pecan Chicken
107

TJ's Terrific Turkey Meatballs
107

Fourth of July fireworks explode in a rainbow of colors behind the U.S. Pavilion in Riverfront Park.
Photograph courtesy of The Spokesman-Review.

Grilled Prime Rib of Beef with Garlic and Rosemary

Roast

1 (16- to 18-pound) beef prime rib
   roast, trimmed and tied
6 to 8 garlic cloves, cut into
   quarters lengthwise
6 to 8 sprigs of fresh rosemary

Rub

2 tablespoons peppercorns
2 tablespoons dried rosemary
2 tablespoons coarse salt
   (kosher or sea salt)
2 tablespoons sweet paprika

Set up the grill up for indirect cooking and place a large drip pan in the center. Preheat to medium. Light only the outside burners, if possible.

For the roast, make several 1/2-inch-deep slits in the roast 2 inches apart, focusing on the top layer of fat. Insert the garlic pieces into half of the holes. Strip the leaves from 2 to 3 of the rosemary sprigs and insert them into the remaining holes. Slide the remaining sprigs under the kitchen twine used to tie the roast.

For the rub, grind the peppercorns and rosemary to a fine powder in a spice mill or blender. Add the salt and paprika and grind to mix. Press the mixture over the surface of the roast, focusing on the top layer of fat.

Arrange the roast in a large disposable aluminum roasting pan. Grill, covered, for 12 to 14 minutes per pound (about 3 1/2 to 4 hours) for medium-rare or until a meat thermometer registers 145 degrees (or 160 degrees for medium). Let stand for 30 minutes before carving.

Note: The internal temperature of the roast will rise about 2 degrees after it is removed from the heat.

Serves 12 to 16

To carve a bone-in prime rib roast, begin cutting bone side up to separate the meat from the bone. Cut the meat into slices as thick or thin as you like.

PJ's Prime Rib Roast

1 (5- to 6-pound) rib roast
1/2 cup vodka
Olive oil
Bay leaves
Sea salt
Granulated garlic
Dried thyme
Pepper
Celery salt

Make slits 1 inch apart on top of the roast. Place the roast in a sealable plastic bag. Pour the vodka over the roast; seal the bag. Let stand at room temperature for 1 hour.

Preheat the oven to 450 degrees. Remove the roast from the bag and pat dry. Coat the roast with olive oil. Press bay leaves into the slits in the roast. Season the roast with sea salt, garlic, thyme, pepper and celery salt. Arrange the roast on a rack in a roasting pan. Roast for 30 minutes. Reduce the heat to 325 degrees and roast for 15 minutes per pound or until a meat thermometer registers 145 degrees for medium-rare or 160 degrees for medium. Let stand for 20 minutes before carving.

Serves 8 to 10

Don't be afraid to make this dish at home. With this recipe, you won't need to go out any longer to have wonderful prime rib.

Sizzling Summer Sirloins

6 tablespoons red wine vinegar
2 tablespoons brown sugar
1/2 cup soy sauce
6 tablespoons Asian sesame oil
2 (1 1/2-pound) sirloin steaks,
    cut 1 inch thick
Chopped parsley (optional)
Sprigs of fresh rosemary

Combine the vinegar, brown sugar, soy sauce and sesame oil in a glass baking dish and mix well. Add the steaks, turning to coat with the marinade. Marinate in the refrigerator for 6 hours or longer, turning occasionally. Preheat the grill to high. Grill the steaks for 5 minutes per side for medium-rare. Sprinkle with parsley and garnish with rosemary sprigs.

Serves 6

Serve these with Sweet Onion Rings, page 82.

Beef Tenderloin with Cranberries

1 (3-pound) beef tenderloin
1 cup dried cranberries
1 cup cranberry juice
1 cup tawny port
3 tablespoons brown sugar
2 tablespoons soy sauce
1 teaspoon coarsely ground
   black pepper or lemon pepper
1/4 teaspoon salt
3 garlic cloves, minced
1 tablespoon all-purpose flour

Place the tenderloin in a large sealable plastic bag. Combine the cranberries, cranberry juice, port, brown sugar, soy sauce, pepper, salt and garlic in a bowl and mix well. Pour over the tenderloin; seal the bag. Marinate in the refrigerator for 24 hours, turning occasionally. Remove the tenderloin from the marinade, reserving the marinade.

Preheat the oven to 500 degrees. Arrange the tenderloin in a roasting pan coated with nonstick cooking spray and place in the oven. Reduce the temperature to 350 degrees. Roast for 1 hour or until a meat thermometer registers 140 degrees for rare or 160 degrees for medium. Let stand for 10 minutes.

Combine the flour and 2 tablespoons of the reserved marinade in a medium saucepan, whisking until smooth. Add the remaining marinade and heat to boiling. Cook until thick, stirring constantly. Serve warm with the beef.

Serves 6 to 8

Lime-Grilled Flank Steak

1 1/2 pounds beef flank steak
1/3 cup red wine vinegar
2 large garlic cloves, crushed
2 tablespoons Dijon mustard
3 tablespoons chopped cilantro
1/4 teaspoon crushed red pepper
1 tablespoon fresh lime juice
   Lime slices

Combine the steak, vinegar, garlic, mustard, cilantro, red pepper and lime juice in a glass dish or sealable plastic bag. Marinate in the refrigerator for 4 hours, turning occasionally.

Preheat the grill to medium-high. Remove the steak from the marinade, discarding the marinade. Grill the steak for about 6 minutes per side or to the desired degree of doneness. Let stand for 10 minutes. Thinly slice the steak against the grain. Garnish with lime slices.

Serves 4

Chili-Rubbed Flank Steak

1 large garlic clove
1 tablespoon chopped red onion
  Zest of 1 lime
1 tablespoon fresh lime juice
2 teaspoons chili powder
2 teaspoons salt
1 teaspoon ground cumin
1 tablespoon olive oil
1 1/2 pounds beef flank steak
2 limes, cut into wedges
1 cup (4 ounces) shredded
  Monterey Jack cheese
2 tablespoons chopped cilantro
12 (6-inch) corn tortillas (optional)

Pulse the garlic, onion, lime zest, lime juice, chili powder, salt and cumin in a food processor until smooth. Add the olive oil in a fine stream, processing constantly until the mixture reaches a paste consistency. Rub the paste over both sides of the steak. (At this point, the steak may be refrigerated for up to 1 1/2 days until ready to cook.)

Preheat the grill to medium-high. Grill the steak for 5 to 6 minutes per side for medium-rare or until a meat thermometer registers 145 degrees. Let stand for 10 minutes. Slice the steak against the grain into 1/4-inch slices.

Arrange the steak on a warm platter. Squeeze one lime wedge over the steak and top with the cheese and cilantro. Serve with warm tortillas and the remaining lime wedges.

Serves 4

3R Party Brisket

1 (14-ounce) can beef broth
1 (4-ounce) bottle liquid smoke
1/4 cup Worcestershire sauce
1 tablespoon dark brown sugar
1 tablespoon hot red pepper sauce
  All-purpose flour
1 (5-pound) top-cut beef brisket
1 large onion, sliced

Combine the broth, liquid smoke, Worcestershire sauce, brown sugar and hot sauce in a medium bowl and mix well. Pierce a large roasting bag and coat with flour using the package directions. Place the brisket fat side up in the bag and arrange in a shallow baking dish just large enough to hold it. Scatter the onion over the brisket. Pour the broth mixture slowly over all sides of the brisket; seal the bag. Let stand at room temperature for 1 hour. Preheat the oven to 325 degrees. Roast the brisket for 4 hours or until very tender. Let stand for 10 minutes. Remove the brisket from the bag, discarding the onion and cooking liquid. Thinly slice the brisket against the grain. Serve immediately.

Serves 8

Tacos al Carbon

1¹/2 cups thinly sliced red bell peppers
1 tablespoon olive oil
1¹/2 cups thinly sliced onions
1 pound beef flank steak, trimmed
  and thinly sliced
1 tablespoon chili powder
1 tablespoon fresh lime juice
³/4 teaspoon salt
4 garlic cloves, minced
8 (6-inch) flour tortillas or
  corn tortillas
3 tablespoons chopped fresh cilantro
1 cup (4 ounces) shredded Mexican
  or Cheddar cheese
6 tablespoons sour cream

Sauté the bell peppers in the olive oil in a grill pan over medium-high heat for 4 minutes. Add the onions. Sauté for 10 minutes or until the vegetables are tender. Remove to a bowl and keep warm. Place the steak in the grill pan over high heat. Cook for 6 to 8 minutes or to the desired degree of doneness. Add the steak to the onion mixture. Add the chili powder, lime juice, salt and garlic to the bowl and toss to coat.

Warm the tortillas using the package directions. Place a heaping spoonful of the steak mixture on each tortilla. Top with cilantro, cheese and sour cream. Fold the tortillas around the filling and enjoy!

Variation: You may substitute chicken breasts or thighs, lamb or shrimp in this south-of-the-border recipe.

Serves 8

Slow-Cooker French Dip

1 (3-pound) beef roast
2 cups water
¹/2 cup soy sauce
1 tablespoon dried rosemary
2 teaspoons thyme
2 teaspoons garlic powder
2 bay leaves
6 to 10 peppercorns
  French rolls
  Softened butter

Combine the roast, water, soy sauce, rosemary, thyme, garlic powder, bay leaves and peppercorns in a slow cooker and mix well. Cook on High for 6 to 7 hours or until the roast is tender. Remove the roast from the liquid, reserving the liquid. Shred the roast and set aside. Split the rolls and spread with butter. Broil or toast until brown. Pile the rolls with the shredded roast. Remove the bay leaves and peppercorns from the cooking liquid and use as a dipping sauce.

Serves 6 to 8

This is destined to become a family favorite!

Marvelous Muffulettas

1 (1-pound) round loaf of bread
1/4 cup red wine vinegar
2 garlic cloves, minced
1 teaspoon dried oregano
1/3 cup olive oil
10 large mixed olives, chopped
1/3 cup chopped pitted
    kalamata olives
1/4 cup chopped roasted red
    bell pepper
    Salt to taste
    Freshly ground pepper to taste
4 ounces thinly sliced ham
4 ounces thinly sliced turkey
4 ounces thinly sliced salami or
    other deli meat
4 ounces sliced provolone cheese
1/2 red onion, thinly sliced
1 1/2 ounces fresh basil or
    spinach leaves

Cut the top third from the loaf of bread and set aside. Hollow out the bottom and top halves of the bread.

Whisk the vinegar, garlic and oregano in a bowl until smooth. Whisk in the olive oil gradually. Stir in the olives and bell pepper. Season with salt and pepper to taste. Spread some of the olive mixture over the bread bottom and cut side of the bread top.

Layer the ham, turkey, salami and cheese in the bread bottom. Top with the onion, basil and the remaining olive mixture. Cover carefully with the bread top. Serve immediately, or wrap tightly in plastic wrap and chill in the refrigerator. To serve, cut into thin wedges.

Serves 6 to 8

This perfectly portable giant sandwich goes anywhere— tailgating, to the lake, or picnicking in the park.

Spokane Centennial Trail

The people of Spokane are proud of the natural beauty of the surrounding area in which we live. A great way to appreciate and experience the beauty of Spokane is visiting the lovely Centennial Trail. The Trail is a paved thirty-seven-mile stretch along the Spokane River. It goes from the Idaho state line to Nine Mile Falls just north of Spokane. People are free to walk, run, skate, bike, or find a sunny spot to soak up the lovely view of the Spokane River flowing by. (See www.spokanecentennialtrail.org.) The Trail is maintained by state, county, and city agencies, as well as a private nonprofit group. It is another great way that Spokane shows its appreciation for the lovely spot where we are so fortunate to live.

Pork Tenderloin Medallions with Port and Bing Cherry Sauce

2 pounds pork tenderloin, sliced
    into 1/2-inch medallions
    Salt and pepper
1/4 cup olive oil
1 cup port
1/2 cup dried Bing cherries
1 tablespoon unsalted butter
    Fresh rosemary, oregano
    and thyme
    Beef broth
    Wondra flour or cornstarch
    Chopped fresh parsley

Season the medallions with salt and pepper to taste. Heat the olive oil in a large skillet until very hot. Add the medallions. Cook over high heat for about 4 minutes per side or until browned and cooked through. Remove to a platter and keep warm.

Add the port to the skillet. Cook over high heat, stirring and scraping up any browned bits. Add the cherries, butter, rosemary, oregano and thyme and mix well. Cook until reduced by half. Add a little beef broth if the sauce looks dry. Whisk in a small amount of flour or cornstarch mixed with water until blended. Cook until thickened, stirring constantly. Return the medallions to the skillet. Reheat the medallions in the sauce over low heat.

To serve, arrange the medallions on a platter and drizzle with the sauce. Sprinkle with parsley.

Serves 4 to 6

RJ's Barbecue Sauce

1 onion, sliced
1 tablespoon vegetable oil
5 garlic cloves, minced
1/2 cup packed brown sugar
2 cups ketchup
3/4 cup cider vinegar
1/2 cup soy sauce
2 tablespoons Worcestershire sauce
1 teaspoon red pepper flakes
1 teaspoon dry mustard
1 tablespoon black pepper

Sauté the onion in the oil in a saucepan over medium heat for 10 minutes or until tender and golden brown. Add the garlic, brown sugar, ketchup, vinegar, soy sauce, Worcestershire sauce, red pepper flakes, mustard and black pepper and mix well. Simmer over low heat for 30 minutes, stirring occasionally.

Makes about 3 cups

Pork Tenderloins with Herbed Crumb Crust

1 small loaf French bread,
  torn into pieces, or 4 cups
  French bread crumbs
2/3 cup chopped fresh parsley
2 tablespoons chopped
  fresh rosemary
2 tablespoons finely crumbled
  bay leaves
1 teaspoon salt
1/2 teaspoon freshly ground pepper
4 eggs, beaten
4 (1-pound) pork tenderloins
1/4 cup (1/2 stick) butter

Combine the bread, parsley, rosemary, bay leaves, salt and pepper in a blender or food processor and process until the consistency of fine crumbs. Spread the mixture in a shallow baking dish or on a sheet of waxed paper.

Beat the eggs in a large bowl. Dip the tenderloins into the egg mixture and coat with the crumb mixture.

Preheat the oven to 375 degrees. Heat the butter in a large skillet. Working in batches, brown the tenderloins on all sides. Arrange the tenderloins on a rack in a roasting pan. Roast for 30 minutes or until a meat thermometer registers 160 degrees. Let stand for 5 minutes before slicing.

Serves 8 to 10

This dish is perfect for a special dinner, but will still allow you time with your guests.

Asian Grilled Pork Tenderloins

1/2 cup soy sauce
1/2 cup orange juice
2 tablespoons brown sugar
1 teaspoon ground ginger
2 garlic cloves, minced
2 pork tenderloins

Combine the soy sauce, orange juice, brown sugar, ginger and garlic in a shallow dish and mix well. Add the tenderloins, turning to coat. Chill, covered, in the refrigerator for 8 hours or longer, turning occasionally.

Grill over hot coals for 12 to 15 minutes or until a meat thermometer registers 160 degrees. Let stand for 5 to 10 minutes before slicing.

Serves 4 to 6

Dry-Rubbed Baby Back Ribs with Molasses Barbecue Sauce

Rub and Ribs

  8 pounds baby back ribs, trimmed
  1 tablespoon paprika
  1 tablespoon ground cumin
  1 tablespoon salt
  2 teaspoons garlic powder
  2 teaspoons onion powder
  2 teaspoons pepper
  1 teaspoon thyme
  1 teaspoon oregano

Molasses Barbecue Sauce

    1 tablespoon butter
  1/2 cup chopped onion
    1 large garlic clove, minced
    1 cup ketchup
    6 tablespoons molasses
    1 tablespoon brown sugar
    3 tablespoons Worcestershire sauce
    3 tablespoons cider vinegar
    2 teaspoons prepared mustard
  1/4 teaspoon thyme
  3/4 teaspoon liquid smoke
      Salt and pepper to taste

For the ribs, cut each rack into halves, if desired. Combine the paprika, cumin, salt, garlic powder, onion powder, pepper, thyme and oregano in a bowl and mix well. Rub or pat the spice mixture over both sides of the ribs. Place in a large shallow baking dish. Chill, covered, in the refrigerator for 2 hours or overnight.

For the sauce, heat the butter in a saucepan. Add the onion and sauté until tender. Add the garlic and sauté for 1 minute. Stir in the ketchup, molasses, brown sugar, Worcestershire sauce, vinegar, mustard, thyme, liquid smoke, salt and pepper. Reduce the heat to medium and bring to a boil. Cook until thickened, stirring frequently. Remove from the heat and let cool. Preheat the oven to 300 degrees. Arrange the ribs in a single layer in two roasting pans. Bake for 2 hours or until the ribs are cooked through and tender. Brush the sauce over the ribs during the last 30 minutes of baking.

Serves 4 to 6

Curried Pork and Onion Skewers with Mango Pineapple Salsa

Mango Pineapple Salsa

- 3 large mangoes, chopped
- 1 pound tomatillos, husked, rinsed and chopped
- 1 cup chopped fresh cilantro
- 2 tablespoons chopped jalapeño chiles
- 2 tablespoons lime juice
- 2 garlic cloves, minced
- 2 cups chopped pineapple

Mango Curry Marinade

- 4 cups plain yogurt
- 2 cups chopped fresh cilantro
- 1 cup chopped red onion
- 1 cup mango chutney
- 1 tablespoon curry powder

Pork Skewers

- 4 1/2 pounds pork tenderloin, cut into 2-inch pieces
- 4 red onions, cut into wedges

For the salsa, combine the mangoes, tomatillos, cilantro, jalapeño chiles, lime juice and garlic in a large bowl and mix well. Chill, covered, in the refrigerator for 12 to 24 hours. Stir in the pineapple just before serving.

For the marinade, combine the yogurt, cilantro, onion, chutney and curry powder in a bowl and mix well. Pour the mixture into a sealable plastic bag. Add the pork, turning to coat; seal the bag. Marinate in the refrigerator for 12 to 24 hours.

For the skewers, remove the pork from the marinade, discarding the marinade. Skewer the pork chunks alternately with the onion wedges.

Preheat the grill to medium-high. Grill for 10 minutes or until the pork is browned and cooked through.

Serve the skewers with the salsa.

Serves 10 to 12

Pork Chops with Northwest Mushrooms

1/2 cup all-purpose flour
1 tablespoon seasoned salt
6 center-cut pork chops
1 tablespoon olive oil
1 teaspoon celery salt
2 teaspoons freshly ground pepper
1/4 cup dry white wine
2 cups Northwest mushrooms
(such as chanterelles or shiitakes)
1 cup chopped green onions
4 garlic cloves, minced
1 3/4 cups dry white wine
1/2 cup white wine vinegar

Preheat the oven to 325 degrees.

Combine the flour and seasoned salt in a shallow dish and mix well. Dip the chops into the mixture, turning to coat. Heat the olive oil in a large skillet over medium-high heat. Add the chops and brown for about 7 minutes per side. Season with the celery salt and pepper. Remove to a baking dish.

Pour 1/4 cup wine into the skillet, stirring and scraping up any browned bits. Add the mushrooms, green onions and garlic and mix well. Reduce the heat and sauté for 5 minutes.

Pour 1 3/4 cups wine and the vinegar into the skillet and simmer for 5 minutes. Pour over the chops in the baking dish. Bake, covered, for 1 hour.

Serves 6

Chanterelles are among the top three wild mushrooms, along with morels and porcini. Their mild apricot flavor and full meaty texture make them a favorite among gourmet chefs. Chanterelles are native to the Pacific Northwest.

Apricot-Glazed Pork Chops

Apricot Glaze

16 dried apricots
1¹/₂ cups (12 ounces) apricot nectar
³/₄ cup sugar
¹/₂ cup white vinegar
¹/₂ cup water
1 tablespoon Asian chili
garlic sauce
1 teaspoon salt
¹/₃ cup minced fresh gingerroot
3 garlic cloves, minced
2 tablespoons sesame seeds, toasted
2 green onions, minced
¹/₄ cup chopped cilantro

Chops and Brine

3 tablespoons sea salt
1 cup hot water
6 thick-cut boneless pork
loin chops

For the glaze, combine the apricots, nectar, sugar, vinegar, ¹/₂ cup water, the chili sauce, salt, gingerroot and garlic in a saucepan and mix well. Bring to a boil over low heat; immediately reduce to a simmer. Cook, covered, for 30 minutes, stirring frequently. Remove from the heat and let cool to room temperature. Purée the mixture in a blender or food processor until very smooth.

Stir in the sesame seeds, green onions and cilantro. Chill, covered, in the refrigerator. (This recipe makes a large amount of glaze. Without the green onions and cilantro, the mixture can be stored indefinitely in the refrigerator. Just add the green onions and cilantro prior to use.)

For the brine, combine the sea salt and water in a small bowl and stir until the salt dissolves. Place the chops and brine in a sealable plastic bag; seal the bag. Chill in the refrigerator for 2 to 4 hours. Remove the chops from the brine and pat dry, discarding the brine. Brush the chops with the glaze and arrange on a tray or a baking sheet. Chill in the refrigerator until ready to grill.

Preheat the grill and add mesquite or hickory chips for a smoky flavor. Sear the chops briefly over high heat. Reduce the heat and grill, covered, until the chops are cooked through. Brush with additional glaze, if desired.

Serves 6

Apricots are one of the best natural sources of Vitamin A, especially dried apricots. Vitamin A is essential for healthy skin, good eyesight, and a strong immune system. Apricots are one of the products of the Pacific Northwest.

Black Rock Elk Chops in Huckleberry Port Reduction

Chops and Marinade

  4 (10- to 12-ounce) elk
      chops, frenched
1/4 cup vegetable oil
  1 tablespoon chopped fresh thyme
      Juice from 1/2 orange
1/4 cup port
  1 garlic clove, minced
  3 tablespoons huckleberries

Sauce

11/2 cups port
 20 black peppercorns, crushed
  2 cups veal demi-glace
11/2 cups orange juice
 10 whole fresh thyme stems
  1 cup huckleberries
  1 shallot, minced
  1 garlic clove, minced
1/4 cup apple juice
  2 cinnamon sticks
  1 teaspoon coriander seeds

To Serve

1/4 cup (1/2 stick) unsalted butter
  1 tablespoon vegetable oil
  2 ounces fresh thyme sprigs
  8 unpeeled whole garlic cloves

For the chops, wrap the exposed portion of the bone with foil.

For the marinade, combine the oil, thyme, orange juice, port, garlic and huckleberries in a bowl and mix well. Pour the mixture into a sealable plastic bag. Add the chops, turning to coat; seal the bag. Marinate in the refrigerator for 2 to 4 hours.

For the sauce, combine the port, peppercorns, demi-glace, orange juice, thyme, huckleberries, shallot, garlic, apple juice, cinnamon sticks and coriander seeds in a heavy saucepan and mix well. Bring to a boil and reduce the heat to low. Simmer until the mixture is reduced to a syrupy consistency, stirring frequently. Strain and keep warm.

Preheat the oven to 450 degrees. Remove the chops from the marinade and pat dry, discarding the marinade. Melt the butter with the oil in a large ovenproof skillet. Add the chops. Brown the chops on both sides, basting frequently with butter. Add the thyme sprigs and garlic cloves to the center of the skillet to form a bed. Arrange the chops on top of the thyme and garlic. Roast in the oven for 8 minutes for medium. (The meat will look rarer than it is because of the huckleberries in the marinade.)

Tent the skillet with foil and let stand for 5 minutes. Reheat the sauce for 2 to 3 minutes, stirring frequently.

Place a chop bone side up in the center of each plate and drizzle the sauce around it. Serve with fingerling potatoes and a medley of baby vegetables.

Serves 4

To "french" a chop is to scrape the meat from the end of a chop or rib to expose the bone. A butcher can do this for you.

Camp Jack Lamb Stew, Moroccan Style

2 pounds lamb stew meat
(10 chunks)
Olive oil
Garlic salt and freshly ground
pepper to taste
2 cups (or more) dry white wine
or chicken broth
1/2 cup creamy peanut butter
1/2 cup Dijon mustard
1 cup small pearl onions
2 garlic cloves, chopped
2 (15-ounce) cans whole
white potatoes
1 cup chopped carrots

Brown the lamb in the olive oil in a Dutch oven over medium-high heat. Season with garlic salt and pepper to taste. Remove the lamb to a platter. Add the wine to the Dutch oven and bring to a boil, stirring and scraping up any browned bits. Whisk in the peanut butter and mustard. Simmer until creamy, stirring constantly. Add the onions, garlic, potatoes and carrots and bring to a boil.

Add the lamb and simmer, covered, for 1 1/2 hours or until the lamb is tender. Check the liquid level occasionally, adding more wine or broth if the stew looks too thick. The sauce should be smooth and creamy. Serve the stew in individual serving bowls with warm crusty French bread for dipping.

Note: To complete the meal, make a large Mediterranean salad of greens, cucumbers, Greek olives, feta cheese and tomatoes tossed with a dressing of lemon juice, olive oil and oregano. Serve with a chilled crisp Tavel dry rosé wine.

Serves 4 to 6

The author of this recipe once had a conversation with the French-Algerian owner of the old A La Parisienne Restaurant that was located in downtown Spokane after Expo 74. He confided that the real way to cook lamb was the way the Berbers do it in the far reaches of the Sahara Desert—slowly simmered with hints of Dijon mustard and peanut flavors. This recipe is an occasional alternative to the more traditional Irish stew.

Chicken with Bacon, Mushrooms and Spinach

4 large boneless skinless
   chicken breasts
3 tablespoons olive oil
2 cups sliced white mushrooms
1/2 cup chopped onion
4 slices smoked bacon or pepper
   bacon, chopped
1/2 teaspoon garlic (fresh or
   from a jar)
1/4 cup dry white wine
1/2 cup chicken stock or broth
1 tablespoon cornstarch
3/4 cup heavy cream
4 cups baby spinach leaves

Sauté the chicken in the olive oil in a large skillet over medium-high heat for 5 to 7 minutes per side or until cooked through. Remove the chicken to a platter. Add the mushrooms, onion, bacon and garlic to the skillet. Sauté over medium-high heat until the onion is soft and the bacon begins to crisp. Add the wine and stock, stirring and scraping up any browned bits. Simmer until reduced by half. Whisk the cornstarch and cream in a small bowl until smooth. Stir the cornstarch mixture into the wine in the skillet. Return the chicken to the skillet. Simmer until ready to serve.

To serve, spread the spinach on a large serving platter and top with the chicken and the sauce. This dish goes well with mashed potatoes, orzo or rice.

Tip: This is a very adaptable recipe. Cut the chicken into small pieces, and you'll have a great filling for puff pastry shells or mushroom caps.

Serves 4

Bloomsday

Every spring, on the first Sunday in May, as many as 50,000 Spokane runners, walkers, and joggers don their lucky shoes and head out for the largest timed road race in the world. Since 1977, the Lilac Bloomsday Run has been an annual tradition for young and old alike, attracting world-caliber athletes as well as those who just want to finish a 12K run. The night before, participants all over the city feast on local pasta favorites, hoping that these delicious carbohydrates will provide them with the energy to get through the race. Sometimes the runners are treated to a lovely sunny day, and sometimes they run in the snow and rain. Either way, Bloomsday is an integral part of springtime in Spokane.

Chicken Kiev

1/2 cup fine dry bread crumbs
1/2 cup (2 ounces) grated
    Parmesan cheese
1 teaspoon oregano leaves
1/2 teaspoon garlic salt
1/4 teaspoon pepper
1/4 cup (1/2 stick) butter, softened
1 tablespoon chopped parsley
1/2 teaspoon oregano leaves
4 boneless skinless chicken breasts
4 ounces Pepper Jack cheese,
    cut into strips
5 tablespoons butter, melted

Combine the bread crumbs, Parmesan cheese, 1 teaspoon oregano, the garlic salt and pepper in a shallow dish and mix well.

Combine 1/4 cup butter, the parsley and 1/2 teaspoon oregano in a small bowl and mix well. Pound the chicken to a uniform thickness between sheets of waxed paper. Spread 1/2 teaspoon of the butter mixture across each chicken piece. Lay 1 strip of Pepper Jack cheese in the center of each chicken piece. Roll the chicken around the filling and tuck in the ends. Dip the chicken in the melted butter and coat evenly with the bread crumb mixture. Place the chicken seam side down, several inches apart, in a 9×13-inch baking dish. Drizzle with any remaining butter. Chill, covered, in the refrigerator for 4 hours or longer.

Preheat the oven to 325 degrees. Bake, uncovered, for 20 minutes or until cooked through.

Serves 4

Honey Lime Chicken

1/2 teaspoon ground ginger
1/2 teaspoon garlic salt
1/4 teaspoon pepper
4 boneless skinless chicken breasts
2 cups julienned carrots
1 red bell pepper, julienned
1/2 cup honey
3 tablespoons fresh lime juice
1 tablespoon soy sauce
    Hot cooked rice or pasta

Preheat the oven to 450 degrees. Combine the ginger, garlic salt and pepper in a small bowl and mix well. Arrange the chicken in a 9×13-inch baking dish and sprinkle with the ginger mixture. Top with the carrots and bell pepper. Whisk the honey, lime juice and soy sauce in a bowl until blended. Spoon the honey mixture over the chicken.

Cover with foil and bake for 25 minutes. Serve over rice or pasta.

Serves 4

Ginger-Marinated Chicken

2 cups vegetable oil
2 cups soy sauce
1 cup lemon juice
3 garlic cloves
1/2 cup dried onion
1/2 teaspoon pepper
1 teaspoon ground ginger
8 to 10 boneless skinless
chicken breasts

Combine the oil, soy sauce, lemon juice, garlic, dried onion, pepper and ginger in a blender or food processor and process until blended. Place the chicken in a sealable plastic bag. Pour the marinade into the bag, turning to coat the chicken. Seal the bag and marinate in the refrigerator overnight. Remove the chicken, reserving the marinade. Grill the chicken over medium-hot coals until cooked through, basting occasionally with the marinade.

Serves 8 to 10

Crispy Pub Mustard Chicken

1/2 cup (1 stick) butter
2 garlic cloves, minced
3 tablespoons pub mustard or any
other specialty mustard
1 cup (4 ounces) freshly grated
Parmesan cheese
2 cups Italian-style bread crumbs
1/3 cup chopped parsley (optional)
6 boneless skinless chicken breasts

Melt the butter with the garlic in a small saucepan over medium heat. Simmer the mixture, being careful not to let it burn. Whisk in the mustard until blended. Remove from the heat and let cool slightly.

Preheat the oven to 350 degrees. Combine the cheese, bread crumbs and parsley in a shallow dish and mix well. Dip the chicken in the mustard sauce and dredge in the cheese mixture, coating both sides. Arrange the chicken in a 9×13-inch baking dish coated with nonstick cooking spray. Bake for 30 minutes or until cooked through.

Serves 6

Pub mustard is an easy-to-prepare British condiment. Just combine 2 cups dry mustard, 1 cup packed brown sugar, 2 teaspoons salt, 1/2 teaspoon turmeric and 12 ounces flat strong ale in a bowl and mix well. Store in the refrigerator in a tightly sealed container.

Chicken Joseph

Chicken

- 10 boneless skinless chicken breasts
- 1/2 teaspoon Dijon mustard
- 1 pound cream cheese, softened
- 2/3 cup Swiss cheese
- 1/2 cup blue cheese

Sauce

- 1/4 cup (1/2 stick) butter
- 1/4 cup all-purpose flour
- 2 cups chicken broth
- 4 ounces cream cheese, softened
  Chopped parsley (optional)

For the chicken, preheat the oven to 350 degrees. Pound the chicken pieces to 1/4 inch thick between sheets of waxed paper. Brush the chicken pieces with a thin layer of Dijon mustard. Combine the cream cheese, Swiss cheese and blue cheese in a bowl and mix well.

Top each chicken piece with one-tenth of the cream cheese mixture. Roll the chicken around the filling. Tuck the ends under and secure with a wooden pick. Arrange the chicken in a baking dish. Bake for 40 minutes or until cooked through.

For the sauce, melt the butter in a saucepan over medium heat. Whisk in the flour until smooth. Add the broth and cook until thickened, stirring constantly. Add the cream cheese and cook until smooth, stirring constantly.

To serve, spoon the sauce over the baked chicken. Garnish with chopped parsley. Serve with gewürztraminer wine.

Makes 10 servings

Chicken Breasts with Prosciutto and Sage

6 boneless skinless chicken breasts
6 thin slices prosciutto
6 tablespoons Parmesan cheese
3 fresh sage leaves
3 tablespoons (about)
    all-purpose flour
3 tablespoons butter
1 tablespoon olive oil
2 chicken bouillon cubes, crushed
1 cup (or more) dry white wine
    Salt and freshly ground pepper
    to taste
1 cup heavy cream

Pound the chicken to 1/4 inch thick between sheets of waxed paper. Place 1 slice of prosciutto, 1 tablespoon of the Parmesan cheese and 1/2 sage leaf over each chicken piece. Roll the chicken around the filling and secure with a wooden pick or tie with kitchen string.

Place the flour in a shallow dish. Roll the chicken in the flour to coat lightly.

Melt the butter with the olive oil in a large heavy skillet over medium-high heat until the butter foams. Add the chicken. Cook until golden brown on each side. Add the bouillon cubes and 1/2 cup wine to the skillet, stirring constantly. Season with salt and pepper.

Simmer until the wine is reduced by half. Reduce the heat and simmer, covered, for 15 to 20 minutes or until the chicken is tender and cooked through. Turn the chicken several times during cooking, adding more wine if the sauce looks dry. Remove the chicken to a warm platter. Increase the heat and add the cream. Simmer until the cream thickens, stirring and scraping up any browned bits with a wooden spoon. Season with salt and pepper to taste. Return the chicken to the skillet, coat with the sauce and serve.

Note: For a slightly thicker sauce, combine 1 tablespoon softened butter with 1 tablespoon flour and whisk into the sauce. Cook for 2 to 3 minutes or until thickened, whisking constantly.

Serves 6

Bourbon Pecan Chicken

Pecan Chicken

- 1/2 cup finely chopped pecans
- 1/2 cup dry bread crumbs
- 2 tablespoons clarified butter, melted
- 8 boneless skinless chicken breasts
- 2 tablespoons clarified butter, melted

Bourbon Sauce

- 1/4 cup Dijon mustard
- 1/4 cup packed dark brown sugar
- 2 2/3 tablespoons bourbon
- 2 tablespoons soy sauce
- 1 teaspoon Worcestershire sauce
- 3/4 cup (1 1/2 sticks) unsalted butter, chilled and cut into small cubes

For the chicken, combine the pecans, bread crumbs, and 2 tablespoons clarified butter in a small bowl and mix well. Spread the mixture on a plate. Press the chicken into the mixture to coat on both sides. Heat 2 tablespoons clarified butter in a large skillet over medium heat. Place the chicken in the skillet. Fry on both sides until golden brown and cooked through.

For the sauce, whisk the mustard, brown sugar, bourbon, soy sauce and Worcestershire sauce in a small saucepan until smooth. Bring to a simmer over medium-low heat. Remove from the heat and whisk in the butter one piece at a time.

To serve, arrange the chicken on a serving platter and pour the sauce over the top.

Serves 8

TJ's Terrific Turkey Meatballs

- 1 1/2 pounds ground turkey
- 1 (7-ounce) jar pesto (homemade or purchased)
- 1 1/2 slices dry bread, crumbled
- 1 teaspoon salt
- 1/2 teaspoon pepper
- 1 (15-ounce) can tomato sauce
- 1 tablespoon minced dried onions
  Hot cooked pasta
- 1/2 cup (2 ounces) grated Parmesan cheese

Combine the turkey, pesto, bread crumbs, salt and pepper in a bowl and mix well. Warm the tomato sauce and dried onions in a large skillet over medium heat. Shape the turkey mixture into individual meatballs using a small ice cream scoop or spoon and place in the skillet with the sauce. Cook, covered, for 15 minutes. Turn the meatballs and reduce the heat. Cook for 10 minutes longer or until the meatballs are cooked through. Serve over pasta and sprinkle with the cheese.

Serves 4

From Fields & Waters

PASTA & SEAFOOD

Crab is a popular area food that is best eaten straight off the boat.
Photograph courtesy of The Spokesman-Review.

Linguini with Asparagus, Prosciutto and Smoked Mozzarella

1 pound asparagus, trimmed
12 ounces fresh linguini
3 garlic cloves, minced
3 tablespoons olive oil
Salt to taste
Freshly ground pepper to taste
6 ounces thinly sliced prosciutto, cut into strips
6 ounces fresh smoked mozzarella cheese, diced (about 1 cup)
1/4 cup fresh basil, thinly sliced

Cook the asparagus in a large pot of boiling water for 2 to 3 minutes or until tender-crisp. Remove the asparagus with tongs and plunge into ice water to stop the cooking; drain. Cut into 1-inch pieces and set aside.

Return the water to a boil. Add the linguini and cook for 6 minutes or until al dente. Drain, reserving 1 cup of the cooking liquid.

Sauté the garlic in the olive oil in a large heavy skillet over medium heat for 20 seconds or until fragrant. Add the asparagus and mix well. Season with salt and pepper to taste. Add the pasta and some of the reserved cooking liquid if needed. Toss to coat. Add the prosciutto, cheese and basil, tossing to coat. Remove from the heat and serve immediately.

Note: Fresh smoked mozzarella cheese is available in the deli section of better supermarkets.

Serves 4 to 6

Sun-Dried Tomato and Basil Pasta

1 1/2 cups sun-dried tomatoes
8 garlic cloves, minced
15 fresh basil leaves, chopped
1 teaspoon salt
1/2 teaspoon pepper
2/3 cup light olive oil
2 pounds penne pasta, cooked and drained
1 cup (4 ounces) freshly grated Parmesan cheese

Soak the sun-dried tomatoes in hot water until soft; drain. Place the sun-dried tomatoes, garlic, basil, salt, pepper and olive oil in a food processor and process to a paste consistency.

Combine the tomato mixture with the hot cooked pasta in a large bowl and toss to combine. Sprinkle with the cheese and toss again.

Serve warm or at room temperature.

Serves 8 to 10

Chicken with Linguini and Peanut Sauce

Peanut Sauce

- 1/2 cup peanut butter
- 1 (14-ounce) can chicken broth
- 2 tablespoons soy sauce
- 1/8 to 1/4 teaspoon ground red pepper
- 2 tablespoons white wine or water
- 1 tablespoon cornstarch

Chicken Linguini

- 1 tablespoon vegetable oil
- 1 sweet onion, thinly sliced
- 2 cloves garlic, minced
- 1 teaspoon grated fresh gingerroot
- 1 pound boneless skinless chicken breasts, cut into 1/2-inch pieces
- 8 ounces linguini, cooked and drained
- 2 green onions, sliced
  Fresh cantaloupe or papaya slices

For the peanut sauce, combine the peanut butter, broth, soy sauce and red pepper in a blender and process until smooth. Pour the mixture into a small saucepan. Whisk the wine and cornstarch in a bowl until blended. Add the cornstarch mixture to the saucepan and mix well. Cook the mixture over low heat until thickened, stirring constantly.

For the chicken, heat the oil in a large skillet or wok over high heat. Separate the onion slices into rings and stir-fry with the garlic and gingerroot for 1 to 2 minutes. Add the chicken and stir-fry for 5 minutes or until cooked through. Add the peanut sauce and linguini, tossing to coat.

To serve, remove to a large platter and garnish with the green onions. Arrange cantaloupe and papaya slices around the edge of the platter. The fruit provides a wonderful contrast to the spicy peanut sauce.

Serves 4 to 6

Jan's Perfect Pesto

- 2 cups loosely packed basil leaves
- 1/2 cup olive oil
- 2 tablespoons butter, softened
- 1/2 cup (2 ounces) grated Parmesan cheese
- 2 tablespoons grated Romano cheese
- 3 tablespoons pine nuts
- 1/2 teaspoon salt
- 2 garlic cloves, minced

Combine the basil, olive oil, butter, Parmesan cheese, Romano cheese, pine nuts, salt and garlic in a blender or food processor and process until smooth. There should still be some texture remaining from the pine nuts, basil and Parmesan cheese. The pesto may be used immediately, refrigerated for 1 to 2 weeks or frozen for up to 1 year.

Makes 1 cup

Pasta Russo

4 to 5 garlic cloves, minced
1/4 teaspoon crushed red
   pepper flakes
2 tablespoons olive oil
2 red bell peppers, julienned
1 yellow bell pepper, julienned
3/4 cup sun-dried tomatoes, sliced
1 pound peeled shrimp or
   diced chicken
1 pound penne
1 cup broccoli florets
   Freshly grated Parmesan cheese

Sauté the garlic and red pepper flakes in the olive oil in a large heavy skillet or wok until the garlic is golden brown; do not burn. Add the bell peppers, sun-dried tomatoes and shrimp or chicken. Cook until the vegetables are soft and the shrimp are pink, or the chicken is browned and cooked through.

Cook the pasta in a pot of boiling water for 8 to 10 minutes or until al dente. Add the broccoli to the pasta water during the last 5 minutes of cooking; drain. Place the pasta and broccoli in a large bowl and add the shrimp mixture. Toss to combine. Spoon into individual serving bowls and top with Parmesan cheese.

Serves 4 to 6

Bow Ties with Palomino Sauce

1 tablespoon butter
1 cup chopped onion
1 banana pepper or other mild
   pepper, chopped
2 garlic cloves, chopped
1 tablespoon all-purpose flour
3/4 cup milk
1/2 cup heavy cream
1/2 teaspoon salt
1 1/4 cups spaghetti sauce
1 pound bow tie pasta, cooked
   and drained
1/2 cup (2 ounces) grated
   Parmesan cheese
1/3 cup sliced fresh basil leaves

For the sauce, melt the butter in a 12-inch nonstick skillet over medium heat. Add the onion, pepper and garlic. Sauté until the vegetables are tender. Stir in the flour; cook for 1 minute. Stir in the milk, cream and salt. Bring to a boil over medium-high heat, stirring constantly. Stir in the spaghetti sauce. Cook over medium-high heat until heated through, stirring occasionally.

Serve the sauce over the hot cooked pasta. Toss with the cheese and basil. Serve immediately.

Note: Banana peppers are mild peppers that are easily confused with hotter yellow wax peppers. If in doubt, choose a yellow bell pepper.

Serves 4 to 6

Pasta with Pumpkin, Sage and Sausage

1 pound bulk sweet Italian sausage
2 tablespoons extra-virgin olive oil
4 garlic cloves, minced
1 onion, finely chopped
1 bay leaf
4 to 6 sage leaves, cut into
  chiffonade (about 2 tablespoons)
1 cup dry white wine
1 cup chicken broth
1 cup canned pumpkin
1/2 cup heavy cream
1/8 teaspoon ground cinnamon
1/2 teaspoon freshly ground or
  grated nutmeg
1/4 to 1/2 teaspoon red pepper flakes
  Coarse salt and black pepper
  to taste
1 pound penne, cooked and
  drained
  Grated Romano or Parmesan
  cheese
  Sage leaves
  Pumpernickel or whole
  grain bread

Brown the sausage in 1 tablespoon of the olive oil in a deep nonstick skillet over medium-high heat, stirring until crumbly and cooked through; drain. Remove to a paper towel-lined plate. Add the remaining 1 tablespoon olive oil to the skillet. Add the garlic and onion and sauté over medium-high heat for 3 to 5 minutes or until the onion is tender.

Add the bay leaf, sage and wine. Simmer for 2 minutes or until the wine is reduced by half. Add the broth and pumpkin and mix well. Cook until the mixture begins to bubble, stirring frequently. Return the sausage to the skillet and stir in the cream. Add the cinnamon, nutmeg and red pepper flakes and mix well. Season with salt and black pepper to taste. Simmer for 5 to 10 minutes or until thickened, stirring frequently. Remove the bay leaf from the sauce and discard.

Place the penne in a large stockpot and add the sausage mixture. Cook over low heat for 1 minute, tossing to coat. Remove to a large serving bowl or platter and garnish with grated cheese and sage leaves.

Serve with pumpernickel or whole grain bread.

Note: To make a chiffonade, layer the leaves of the herb to be used in a neat pile and make very thin slices.

Serving Tip: Try this with the Northwest Spinach Salad with Apple and Cheddar (page 75) for an amazing autumn supper.

Serves 4 to 6

Sauce Bolognese

2 tablespoons unsalted butter
2 tablespoons extra-virgin olive oil
1 small onion, diced
1/2 carrot, diced
1 rib celery, diced
8 ounces ground pork
4 ounces ground beef
4 ounces ground veal
4 ounces prosciutto, diced
Salt and pepper to taste
1/2 cup dry white wine
1 (28-ounce) can Italian plum
  tomatoes, crushed and seeded
1 cup chicken broth
1/2 cup milk, warmed

Heat the butter and olive oil in a Dutch oven over medium heat. Add the onion, carrot and celery when the butter begins to foam. Cook for 5 to 7 minutes or until golden and soft, stirring frequently. Increase the heat to high and add the pork, beef, veal and prosciutto. Season with salt and pepper. Cook for 3 to 5 minutes or until the meats are browned and crumbly, stirring frequently. Add the wine and simmer until all the liquid has evaporated. Add the tomatoes and broth, stirring to combine. Bring the mixture to a boil; reduce the heat to low and simmer for 2 hours.

Just before serving, stir in the warm milk. Toss with a favorite pasta.

Serves 8

Lilac Festival and Torchlight Parade

Known as the "Lilac City," Spokane is also the host of the Spokane Lilac Festival and Armed Forces Torchlight Parade. The event was started in 1938 by local garden clubs and the Spokane Floral Society. They wanted to celebrate the stunning array of lilacs blooming throughout the region, as well as the outstanding talent and beauty of local young women. In 1949, with the creation of National Armed Forces Day, the event grew to include the recognition and appreciation of our country's armed forces.

The Lilac Festival and Armed Forces Parade demonstrate the deep-seated partnership between the civilian community of Spokane and nearby Fairchild Air Force Base. For example, after the tragic events September 11, 2001,

(continued on page 115)

Straight Out of the Garden Red Sauce

2½ pounds sweet Italian sausage, casings removed
3 tablespoons olive oil
1½ pounds mushrooms, sliced
3 cups chopped onion
¼ cup fresh oregano leaves
6 cloves garlic, chopped
1 cup fresh basil leaves, sliced
1 cup (4 ounces) Pecorino Romano cheese
1 cup dry white wine
5 cups crushed tomatoes with added purée
2 cups fresh tomatoes, diced
2 tablespoons butter
Salt and pepper
1¼ pounds pappardelle pasta
½ cup (2 ounces) Pecorino Romano cheese
½ cup basil leaves, sliced

Sauté the sausage in the olive oil in a large skillet over medium-high heat until browned and crumbly, stirring constantly; drain. Remove to a paper towel-lined bowl. Sauté the mushrooms and onions until light brown. Stir in the oregano, garlic, 1 cup basil and ½ cup cheese. Cook for 1 minute, stirring constantly. Add the wine and simmer for 4 minutes longer. Return the sausage to the skillet and add the crushed tomatoes. Cover and simmer for 25 minutes or until thick, stirring occasionally. Add the diced tomatoes and butter and simmer for 15 minutes longer. Season with salt and pepper to taste.

Cook the pappardelle using the package directions; drain. Place the pasta in a large serving bowl and cover with the sauce. Toss to coat.

Serves 8 to 10

the Lilac Festival, together with Fairchild Air Force Base and other community organizations, launched "Operation Spokane Heroes." Its purpose was to show our appreciation and recognition of the bravery and essential services that local men and women in police departments, fire departments, and the U.S. military provide on a daily basis. (See www.spokanelilacfestival.org). In 2001, the Lilac Festival Lapel Pin, a perennial part of the festivities, showed the Red Wagon in Riverfront Park (originally donated by the Junior League of Spokane) together with the American flag and lilacs, our city's flower. A New York City fireman and two New York City policemen who worked clearing the wreckage of the World Trade Center buildings spoke during the Festival. For this effort, the Lilac Festival was awarded the Zachary Fischer Award by the United States Air Force. A prestigious national honor, the award is for "recognizing humanitarian efforts of a civilian community to honor a military community."

Roasted Butternut Squash Lasagna

Roasted Butternut Squash

   3 pounds butternut squash, peeled,
      quartered, seeded and cut into
      1/2-inch cubes
   3 tablespoons vegetable oil
      Salt to taste

Béchamel Sauce

   4 cups milk
   1 tablespoon dried rosemary,
      crumbled
   1 tablespoon dried basil, crumbled
 1/4 cup (1/2 stick) unsalted butter
   1 tablespoon minced garlic
 1/4 cup all-purpose flour

Lasagna

   1 (16-ounce) package no-boil
      lasagna noodles
1 1/3 cups grated Parmesan cheese
   1 cup heavy whipping cream
 1/2 teaspoon salt

For the squash, preheat the oven to 450 degrees. Toss the squash with the oil in a large bowl to coat. Spread the squash on two oiled large baking sheets. Roast for 10 minutes; season with salt. Stir and roast for 10 minutes longer or until tender.

For the sauce, combine the milk, rosemary and basil in a saucepan and bring to a simmer. Cook over low heat for 10 minutes, stirring occasionally. Pour the mixture through a fine mesh sieve into a large heatproof bowl.

Melt the butter in a large saucepan over low heat. Add the garlic. Sauté until soft. Whisk in the flour until smooth. Cook for 3 minutes, stirring constantly. Remove from the heat and whisk in the milk mixture slowly until smooth. Return to the heat and simmer gently for 10 minutes or until the sauce has thickened enough to coat the back of a spoon. The sauce can be made ahead and chilled. Cover the surface with plastic wrap.

For the lasagna, reduce the oven temperature to 375 degrees. Spread 1 cup of the sauce in a buttered 9×13-inch baking dish. Cover with three lasagna noodles; the noodles should not touch. Spread half the remaining sauce over the noodles and sprinkle with 1/2 cup of the cheese. Repeat the layering with three lasagna noodles, the remaining sauce and 1/2 cup of the cheese. Top with the remaining lasagna noodles.

Beat the cream and salt in a mixing bowl until soft peaks form. Cover the lasagna with the whipped cream. Sprinkle the remaining 1/3 cup cheese over the cream. Cover the dish tightly with foil (tent slightly to prevent the foil from sticking). Bake for 30 minutes. Remove the foil and bake for 10 minutes longer or until golden brown and bubbly. Let stand for 5 minutes before serving.

Serves 12

Halibut Macadamia with Chive Butter Sauce

Halibut Macadamia

  6 (6-ounce) fresh halibut fillets
 1/3 cup milk
 1/2 teaspoon salt
 1/4 teaspoon pepper
 1/2 cup diced macadamia nuts
 2/3 cup fine dry bread crumbs
  1 tablespoon finely chopped parsley
 1/2 teaspoon paprika
 1/4 cup (1/2 stick) unsalted
      butter, melted
  1 tablespoon fresh lemon juice
  1 tablespoon white wine

Chive Butter Sauce

  1 tablespoon unsalted butter
 1/4 cup finely chopped shallots
 1/4 cup white wine
 1/4 cup heavy cream
 1 1/2 sticks (3/4 cup) plus 3 tablespoons
      unsalted butter, chilled
 1/4 teaspoon white pepper
 1/2 cup finely snipped fresh chives

For the halibut, preheat the oven to 350 degrees. Rinse the halibut and pat dry. Combine the milk, salt and pepper in a shallow dish and mix well. Combine the macadamia nuts, bread crumbs, parsley and paprika in another shallow dish and mix well. Dip the halibut in the milk mixture and coat both sides with the macadamia nut mixture. Arrange in a single layer in a greased 9×13-inch baking dish.

Combine the butter, lemon juice and wine in a bowl and mix well. Drizzle the butter mixture over the fish. Bake for 10 to 15 minutes or until the fish flakes easily.

For the sauce, melt 1 tablespoon butter in a skillet over medium heat. Add the shallots. Sauté until the shallots are translucent. Add the wine and simmer for 1 minute. Whisk in the cream gradually until blended. Cook over low heat, stirring occasionally. Add the remaining butter 1 tablespoon at a time, stirring constantly. Add the white pepper and heat through; do not boil. Stir in the chives just before serving.

To serve, place one halibut filet on each plate and drizzle with the sauce.

Serves 6

The richness of the macadamia nuts and cream complements the fish beautifully. This is a perfect "special occasion" recipe.

Halibut with Citrus Pineapple Salsa

Tequila Marinade

- 1/2 cup fresh lime juice
- 1/4 cup tequila
- 4 garlic cloves
- 1 bunch fresh cilantro, chopped
- 1 tablespoon minced gingerroot
- 1 jalapeño chile, seeded
- 2 tablespoons white vinegar
- 1 tablespoon sugar
- 1 tablespoon salt
- 1 1/2 cups olive oil
- 6 (6-ounce) fresh halibut fillets

Citrus Pineapple Salsa

- 1 Texas Ruby Red grapefruit
- 1 orange
- 1 cup diced pineapple
- 1 small red onion, diced
- 2 tablespoons chopped cilantro
- 1 jalapeño chile, seeded
  and chopped
- 2 teaspoons raspberry vinegar
- 2 teaspoons sugar

For the marinade, combine the lime juice, tequila, garlic, cilantro, gingerroot, jalapeño, vinegar, sugar and salt in a food processor. Pulse three times. Add the olive oil in a steady stream, processing constantly until smooth. Reserve 3/4 cup of the marinade to serve with the halibut.

Place the halibut in a shallow dish and pour the remaining marinade over the top, turning to coat. Cover tightly with plastic wrap and marinate in the refrigerator for 2 to 4 hours.

For the salsa, cut a thick slice off the top and bottom of the grapefruit and place upright on a smooth flat work surface. Thickly slice off the peel in strips, removing the white pith and membrane to reveal the fruit sections. Slice the fruit into sections over a large bowl, letting the sections and any juices drop into the bowl. Repeat the process with the orange. Add the pineapple, onion, cilantro, jalapeño chile, vinegar and sugar and mix well.

Drain the halibut, discarding the marinade. Grill the halibut over medium-high heat for 4 minutes per side or until opaque in the center.

To serve, divide the salsa evenly among six serving plates. Top with the halibut and drizzle with 2 to 3 tablespoons of the reserved marinade.

Serves 6

This dish is loaded with color and flavor. Try it with chicken if you prefer.

Grilled Halibut with Brown Sugar Butter

2 tablespoons brown sugar
1 teaspoon minced garlic
1 tablespoon lemon juice
2 teaspoons soy sauce
2 tablespoons butter
1 pound halibut steaks or fillets

Combine the brown sugar, garlic, lemon juice, soy sauce and butter in a saucepan. Cook over medium heat until the brown sugar dissolves, stirring constantly. Brush the mixture on the halibut, coating both sides.

Grill the halibut over medium-high heat for 4 minutes per side or until opaque in the center.

Serves 4

Honey Coriander-Glazed Salmon

3/4 cup honey
1/4 cup (1/2 stick) butter
1 tablespoon chopped coriander
1/2 tablespoon fresh lemon juice
1 tablespoon prepared mustard
2 garlic cloves, crushed
1 teaspoon parsley, chopped
1 pound fresh salmon
Salt and pepper to taste
Chopped parsley for garnish

Combine the honey, butter, coriander, lemon juice, mustard, garlic and 1 teaspoon parsley in a small saucepan. Cook over medium-low heat until the butter is melted, stirring frequently.

Place the salmon on a foil-lined tray. Season with salt and pepper. Grill over medium-high heat until the salmon flakes easily, basting frequently with the honey mixture. Garnish with chopped parsley.

Serves 4

Mesquite-Broiled Salmon with Pesto

1/2 cup olive oil
1/2 cup vegetable oil
1/4 cup minced garlic
1/3 cup finely chopped basil
Grated zest of 1 lemon
Salt to taste
1/3 cup roasted pine nuts, chopped
2 (8-ounce) wild salmon fillets,
skinned and deboned

Mix the olive oil, vegetable oil, garlic, basil, lemon zest and salt in a bowl. Let stand for 1 hour. Add the pine nuts to the olive oil mixture. Add the salmon to the mixture, turning to coat. Cover tightly with plastic wrap and marinate in the refrigerator for 6 hours. Turn every 2 hours to coat evenly. Drain the salmon, reserving the marinade. Grill over mesquite charcoal for 3 to 4 minutes per side, basting with the reserved marinade.

Serves 2

Spring in Riverfront Park

The history of the Inland Northwest is inextricably entwined with rivers. The Spokane, the Columbia, and the Snake sustained generations of Native Americans, creating a rich culture. The rivers also brought the great explorers, Lewis and Clark, and their pioneering expedition of 1804. The rivers provided food such as salmon and trout, and a means of transportation. Ultimately, the rivers would come to provide energy to the Inland Northwest. The local settlers in the Spokane area built the first electric power plants to harness the energy of the Spokane and the Columbia. To this day, visitors are struck by the natural beauty and splendor of the Spokane Falls and the Spokane River as the clear water rushes and foams over the Falls, right through the heart of the city. That beauty continues to be enjoyed today. The river will always be a source of community pride and concern. Attractions such as the Riverfront Park, the Centennial Trail, and the Bowl and Pitcher State Park line the river and provide hours of enjoyment. Concerns linger over the health of the river and the impact of future development. It is Spokane's goal to be good stewards of our natural surroundings. Plans are in place to ensure the continuing health of this vital natural resource.

Sesame-Crusted Salmon with East-Meets-West Guacamole

East-Meets-West Guacamole

- 2 avocados
- 1 garlic clove, minced
- 2 teaspoons fresh lemon juice
- 1/2 teaspoon grated fresh gingerroot
- 2 teaspoons finely chopped onion
- 2 teaspoons olive oil
- 1/2 to 1 teaspoon prepared wasabi paste, or to taste
- Salt and pepper to taste

Sesame-Crusted Salmon

- 4 (6-ounce) salmon fillets, deboned (with or without skin)
- Salt and pepper to taste
- 1/4 cup black sesame seeds
- 1 to 2 tablespoons olive oil or vegetable oil

For the guacamole, mash the avocados in a bowl with a fork until they are mashed but slightly chunky. Add the garlic, lemon juice, gingerroot, onion, olive oil and wasabi paste and mix well. Season with salt and pepper. This can be prepared in advance and stored in the refrigerator for up to 8 hours. Cover tightly with plastic wrap touching the surface of the guacamole and gently squeeze out any air bubbles.

For the salmon, preheat the oven to 350 degrees. Heat a large nonstick ovenproof skillet over medium to medium-high heat. Pat the salmon fillets dry with a paper towel. Season with salt and pepper. Firmly press 1 tablespoon of the sesame seeds on the top of each fillet.

Add the olive oil to the hot skillet. Place the fillets sesame seed side down in the skillet. Cook for 2 minutes. Turn the fillets and place in the oven for 6 to 8 minutes or just until the salmon is cooked through. It should be firm to the touch but not hard or solid

Serve immediately with a large dollop of the East-Meets-West Guacamole on the side.

Serves 4

Wasabi is a traditional Japanese condiment with a strong spicy heat and an intense green color. It can be found in the Asian section of well-stocked grocery stores and specialty markets. It is quite hot, so use an amount that suits your taste.

Cedar Plank Trout

1 cup Dijon mustard
1 cup honey
1/2 cup balsamic vinegar
Olive oil
4 (6-ounce) trout fillets
Salt and freshly ground
pepper to taste

Soak an untreated cedar plank in water overnight. Drain and pat dry with paper towels. Whisk the mustard, honey and vinegar in a small bowl until blended. Brush the plank with olive oil. Arrange the trout on the plank and season with salt and pepper. Brush the trout with the mustard mixture. Place the plank on a hot grill and close the grill lid. Cook the trout for 8 to 10 minutes or until cooked through.

Serves 4

Fabulous Fish Tacos

Grilled Halibut
4 (6- to 8-ounce) fresh halibut fillets
Extra-virgin olive oil
Salt and pepper to taste
Juice of 1 lime

Guacamole
3 small avocados, sliced
Juice of 1 lemon
2 garlic cloves, minced
1/2 teaspoon cayenne pepper
1 cup plain yogurt
1 teaspoon sea salt
2 plum tomatoes, chopped
2 green onions, thinly sliced

Tacos
12 (6-inch) soft flour tortillas
1 heart of romaine, or 1 head cabbage, shredded

For the halibut, preheat a grill pan to high heat. Drizzle the halibut with olive oil to prevent from sticking. Season the halibut with salt and pepper. Grill for 5 minutes per side or until opaque. Sprinkle the halibut with lime juice and remove to a serving platter. Flake the halibut into large chunks with a fork.

For the guacamole, combine the avocados, lemon juice, garlic, cayenne pepper, yogurt and salt in a blender. Process until smooth. Remove the guacamole to a bowl and stir in the tomatoes and green onions.

For the tacos, heat the tortillas in a hot grill pan or cast-iron skillet until blistered. Place 2 to 3 tablespoons grilled fish on each tortilla. Top with 1 to 2 tablespoons guacamole and a sprinkling of romaine. Fold the tortillas around the filling and enjoy!

Serves 12

This transplant from Mexico is just the ticket for those long winter months.

Cracked Crab with Citrus Butter

Citrus Butter

3/4 cup (1¹/2 sticks) unsalted butter

3 tablespoons orange juice

¹/2 teaspoon grated orange zest

1 tablespoon Dijon mustard
Salt and freshly ground pepper
to taste

Cracked Crab

3 (2- to 2¹/2-pound) fresh
Dungeness crabs, cleaned
and cooked

For the citrus butter, melt the butter in a small saucepan over medium heat. Stir in the orange juice, orange zest, mustard, salt and pepper until blended. Remove from the heat immediately and let stand for 1 hour.

For the crab, cut each crab in half from head to tail using a large heavy knife. Cut each half crosswise into thirds. Crack the claws and legs using a small mallet or hammer. Steam the crabs in a steamer basket over boiling water for 5 to 7 minutes to rewarm if necessary.

To serve, reheat the citrus butter over medium heat in the saucepan, whisking constantly. Pour into a small bowl. Arrange the crab on a platter. Serve immediately with the citrus butter.

Serves 4

Asian Scallops

3/4 cup fresh orange juice

2 tablespoons hoisin sauce

1 tablepoon minced gingerroot

12 large sea scallops
Sea salt to taste

1 tablepoon crushed
coriander seeds

2 teaspoons sesame oil

2 baby bok choy, cut lengthwise
into eighths

2 tablespoons water

Whisk the orange juice, hoisin sauce and gingerroot in a small bowl until blended. Pat the scallops dry and season with salt and coriander seeds.

Heat the sesame oil in a heavy skillet over high heat until hot but not smoking. Add the scallops seasoned side down. Cook for 1¹/2 minutes per side or until opaque. Remove the scallops to a plate and keep warm. Add the bok choy and water to the skillet. Sauté over medium-high heat until the bok choy is wilted. Remove to the plate with the scallops. Add the hoisin mixture to the skillet and bring to a boil over high heat. Reduce the mixture to ¹/3 cup, stirring frequently. To serve, divide the bok choy evenly among four plates. Place three scallops on each plate. Drizzle the sauce over the scallops and bok choy.

Serves 4

Shrimp Creole

2 pounds jumbo shrimp, peeled and deveined
2 tablespoons lemon juice
2 tablespoons Worcestershire sauce
1 teaspoon salt
3 tablespoons butter
1 onion, chopped
1/2 green bell pepper, chopped
1/2 cup chopped celery
1 garlic clove, minced
2 tablespoons all-purpose flour
1 teaspoon sugar
1 teaspoon salt
1/4 teaspoon pepper
4 dashes of Tabasco sauce
1/4 cup canned tomatoes
1 (8-ounce) can tomato sauce
Hot cooked rice

Sprinkle the shrimp with the lemon juice, Worcestershire sauce and 1 teaspoon salt. Melt the butter in a large skillet over low heat. Add the onion, bell pepper, celery and garlic. Cook for 5 minutes, stirring frequently. Mix the flour, sugar, 1 teaspoon salt, the pepper, Tabasco sauce, tomatoes and tomato sauce in a bowl. Add the mixture to the skillet and mix well. Cook for 15 to 20 minutes. Add the shrimp. Cook for 3 to 5 minutes or until the shrimp are pink and cooked through. Serve over rice.

Serves 6 to 8

Wine Part I

Spokane is home to ten independent wineries, reflecting a rich diversity of styles and tastes. Whether you are cooking for a casual meal at home or an elegant formal party, there is a Spokane wine that will complement your meal. All the wineries make the best possible use of the abundant grape crops for which Washington is well known. Latah Creek, established in 1982, is one of Spokane's earliest wineries. Striving to produce wines with minimal processing that showcase the authentic flavors of the fruit, the winery continues to enjoy great success locally and nationally. Noted in the Wine Spectator *as "one of the top producers of Merlot in Washington, Latah Creek also produces highly regarded Cabernet Sauvignon and Johannisberg Riesling, a* Wine Spectator *Top 100 Wine. Grateful Spokane residents are also able to purchase Huckleberry d'Latah and Moscato d'Latah. Arbor Crest is another Spokane winery established in 1982. Featuring wines crafted in a "Bordeaux style, using Washington state fruit," this winery is also doing well nationally, listed in the* Wine Spectator's *list of "50 Great Wine Producers Every Wine Lover Should Know."*

Sumptuous Shrimp in Spicy Cream Sauce

Spicy Cream Sauce

 1 cup low-fat cottage cheese
 1/2 cup low-fat cream cheese
 1 (12-ounce) can evaporated skim milk
 1/4 cup mayonnaise

Spicy Seasoning Mix

 1 1/4 teaspoons sweet paprika
 1 1/4 teaspoons salt
 1 teaspoon onion powder
 1 teaspoon garlic powder
 3/4 teaspoon dried basil
 3/4 teaspoon dry mustard
 3/4 teaspoon dried thyme
 1/2 teaspoon black pepper
 1/4 teaspoon white pepper
 1/4 teaspoon dill weed
 1/8 teaspoon cayenne pepper
 1/8 teaspoon ground nutmeg
 1 pound shrimp, peeled and deveined

Pasta

 1/2 cup chopped onion
 1/4 cup chopped green bell pepper
 1 1/4 cups chicken broth
 2 teaspoons Spicy Seasoning Mix
 1/2 cup chopped onion
 1/2 cup chopped green bell pepper
 2 tablespoons all-purpose flour
 1 cup sliced fresh mushrooms
 1/2 teaspoon minced garlic
 4 cups drained cooked linguini

For the cream sauce, combine the cottage cheese, cream cheese, evaporated milk and mayonnaise in a blender or food processor. Process until smooth.

For the seasoning mix, combine the paprika, salt, onion powder, garlic powder, basil, mustard, thyme, black pepper, white pepper, dill weed, cayenne pepper and nutmeg in a small bowl and mix well. Place the shrimp in a large bowl. Sprinkle the shrimp with 1 tablespoon of the Seasoning Mix and toss to coat.

For the pasta, preheat a large nonstick skillet over high heat for 4 minutes. Add 1/2 cup onion and 1/4 cup bell pepper and mix well. Sauté for 3 minutes or until tender, stirring frequently. Add 1/4 cup of the broth, scraping the bottom of the skillet with a wooden spoon to loosen the browned bits. Cook until the liquid evaporates, stirring frequently. Add 1/4 cup of the broth, 2 teaspoons Seasoning Mix, 1/2 cup onion and 1/2 cup bell pepper and mix well. Cook until the liquid evaporates and the vegetables begin to stick. Add 1/2 cup of the broth and the flour, stirring until the flour is completely absorbed. Cook until of a paste consistency, stirring constantly. Stir in the mushrooms and garlic and spread evenly in the skillet. Cook for 5 minutes, scraping the bottom of the skillet as a crust forms. If the mixture looks like it may burn, add the remaining 1/4 cup broth. Cook until the liquid evaporates.

Add the shrimp and the remaining Seasoning Mix. Cook for 3 to 4 minutes or until the shrimp are pink and cooked through, stirring constantly. Stir in the Cream Sauce. Cook just until the mixture begins to boil, stirring constantly. Add the pasta to the skillet and mix well. Cook until heated through, tossing to combine.

Serves 4 to 6

Sweet Temptations

DESSERTS

*Denotes the desserts featured on the front cover

Cameo (foreground) and Jonagold (background) apples catch the morning light in bins at the Harvest House during the Greenbluff Apple Festival. Photograph courtesy of The Spokesman-Review.

Apple Cranberry Crisp

Oatmeal Topping

1 1/2   cups old-fashioned rolled oats
1 1/3   cups packed dark brown sugar
  1   cup all-purpose flour
1 3/4   teaspoons ground cinnamon
  1/4   teaspoon salt
  1   cup (2 sticks) unsalted butter, softened
  1   cup sliced almonds

Apple Cranberry Filling

  4   pounds tart apples, such as pippin or Granny Smith, peeled, cored, quartered and sliced
  1   (12-ounce) package sweetened dried cranberries
  2/3   cup sugar
  1   tablespoon all-purpose flour
  3/4   teaspoon ground cinnamon
    Vanilla ice cream

Preheat the oven to 375 degrees. Butter a 9×13-inch baking dish or a 3-quart baking dish with 2-inch-deep sides.

For the topping, combine the oats, brown sugar, flour, cinnamon and salt in a bowl and mix well. Add the butter. Rub the butter into the dry ingredients with your fingers until the mixture is the consistency of coarse crumbs. Add the almonds and mix well.

For the filling, combine the apples, cranberries, sugar, flour and cinnamon in a bowl and mix well. Place the apple mixture in the prepared baking dish. Spread the oat mixture evenly over the apple mixture.

Bake for 55 minutes or until the topping is golden brown and the apples are tender. Serve warm or at room temperature with a scoop of vanilla ice cream.

Serves 8 to 10

Dark Chocolate Crème Brûlée

2 cups heavy cream
2 cups half-and-half
8 ounces semisweet chocolate,
  finely chopped
8 egg yolks
1/3 cup plus 8 tablespoons sugar

Preheat the oven to 300 degrees. Combine the cream and half-and-half in a large saucepan. Bring to a boil over medium heat. Reduce the heat to low and whisk in the chocolate. Cook until melted and smooth, whisking constantly. Remove from the heat. Whisk the egg yolks and 1/3 cup sugar in a mixing bowl until smooth. Add the chocolate mixture to the egg yolk mixture slowly, whisking constantly; strain.

Divide the mixture among eight 3/4-cup custard cups. Place the cups in a large baking pan. Add enough hot water to the pan to reach halfway up the sides of the cups. Bake for 50 minutes or until the custards are set. Remove from the water. Chill, covered, in the refrigerator for 4 to 5 hours or overnight.

To serve, sprinkle 1 tablespoon sugar over the top of each custard. Brown with a kitchen torch or broil until browned and bubbly. Serve immediately.

Serves 8

Wine—Part II

Mountain Dome Winery, established in 1984, is the "second largest sparkling house in Washington." Using only Washington State grapes, the label strives to produce the "finest sparkling wine possible." Its distinctive label, featuring bearded gnomes, is a local favorite. Utilizing the Washington Vineyard of Seven Hills, Grande Ronde Cellars (established in 1997) produces mostly red wines that "will continue to improve with aging" in 100 percent French oak barrels. Seven Hill's vineyard was recently recognized as one of the "10 best vineyards in the world" by Wine and Spirits *magazine. The winery also produces a lovely Chardonnay.*

Double-Drizzled Pears

Pears

  6 pears
  3 tablespoons lemon juice
  3 cups water
  1/2 large vanilla bean, split

Chocolate Sauce

  2¹/₂ tablespoons sugar
  2¹/₂ tablespoons baking cocoa
  2 tablespoons water
  2 tablespoons light corn syrup
  1/2 teaspoon vanilla extract

Raspberry Sauce

  1¹/₄ cups frozen unsweetened
       raspberries
  2¹/₂ tablespoons sugar
  1/2 teaspoon cornstarch

For the pears, slice 1/4 inch from the bottom of each pear so it will stand upright. Peel each pear and remove the core from the bottom end, leaving the stem intact. Combine the lemon juice, water and vanilla bean in a Dutch oven. Bring to a boil over medium heat. Add the pears cut side down. Reduce the heat and simmer, covered, for 20 minutes or until the pears are tender. Remove the pears from the cooking liquid and let cool. Discard the cooking liquid.

For the chocolate sauce, combine the sugar and baking cocoa in a saucepan and mix well. Add the water and stir until smooth. Add the corn syrup and mix well. Bring to a boil over medium heat, stirring constantly. Remove from the heat and stir in the vanilla. Pour into a bowl, cover and chill.

For the raspberry sauce, combine the raspberries and sugar in a saucepan. Cook over medium-low heat for 3 minutes or until the sugar dissolves, stirring constantly. Strain the mixture, discard the seeds and return the sauce to the saucepan. Add the cornstarch and stir until dissolved. Bring to a boil over medium heat. Boil for 1 minute or until slightly thickened. Remove from the heat. Pour into a bowl, cover and chill.

To serve, spoon 1 tablespoon raspberry sauce onto each of six dessert plates. Place the pear in the center of the sauce and drizzle each with 1 tablespoon chocolate sauce.

Note: Pears are usually sold while still green because they ripen better off the tree. To speed the process, place in a closed paper bag at room temperature for 3 to 7 days.

Serves 6

Three-Milk Cake

8 eggs
1 1/2 cups sugar
2 cups all-purpose flour
1/4 teaspoon salt
1 tablespoon baking powder
1 (14-ounce) can sweetened condensed milk
1 (12-ounce) can evaporated milk
1 cup heavy cream
1 teaspoon vanilla extract

Preheat the oven to 325 degrees. Combine the eggs and sugar in a large mixing bowl. Beat at medium speed with an electric mixer for 5 to 6 minutes or until smooth and pale yellow. Combine the flour, salt and baking powder in a small bowl and mix well. Add the flour mixture in small increments to the egg mixture, beating well after each addition. Pour into a greased 9×13-inch baking pan.

Bake for 35 to 40 minutes or until a wooden pick inserted into the center comes out clean.

Combine the condensed milk, evaporated milk, cream and vanilla in a bowl and mix well. Pour the milk mixture evenly over the hot cake. Let cool for 15 minutes before serving.

Serve chilled or warm. Serve with fresh huckleberries and whipped cream.

Serves 12

This unique recipe will comfort young and old, conjuring up memories of warm summer evenings on Grandma's porch.

Huckleberry Crumble

Crumb Topping

- 1/2 cup sugar
- 1/3 cup all-purpose flour
- 1/2 teaspoon ground cinnamon
- 1/4 cup (1/2 stick) butter, cut into small pieces

Huckleberry Filling

- 1/4 cup (1/2 stick) butter, softened
- 3/4 cup sugar
- 1 egg
- 1 1/2 cups sifted all-purpose flour
- 2 teaspoons baking powder
- 1/2 teaspoon salt
- 1/2 cup milk
- 2 cups fresh or frozen huckleberries

Preheat the oven to 375 degrees.

For the topping, combine the sugar, flour and cinnamon in a bowl and mix well. Cut the butter into the sugar mixture with a pastry blender until the mixture resembles coarse crumbs.

For the crumble, beat the butter and sugar in a mixing bowl with an electric mixer until light and fluffy. Add the egg and beat until smooth. Sift the flour, baking powder and salt together in another bowl. Add the flour mixture alternately with the milk to the butter mixture, beating well after each addition. Gently fold the huckleberries into the batter. Spread the batter in a greased 8×8-inch baking pan. Sprinkle evenly with the topping. Bake for 45 minutes. Cool slightly before serving.

Serves 8

Rum-Marinated Peaches

- 4 peaches, peeled and halved
- 1/2 cup dark rum
- 8 scoops vanilla ice cream

Combine the peaches and rum in a large bowl and mix well. Marinate for 30 minutes. Drain the peaches, reserving the marinade.

Heat a large skillet over medium-high heat. Place the peaches cut side down in the skillet. Cook gently on both sides. Add the remaining rum marinade to the skillet. Cook down until syrupy.

Remove from the heat and cool for 1 minute. Divide the ice cream evenly among four bowls. Spoon two peach halves into each bowl and drizzle with syrup.

Serves 4

Dark Chocolate Cheesecake with Raspberries and Cream

Crust

2¹/₂ cups chocolate wafer cookies, finely crushed

¹/₂ cup (1 stick) butter, melted

2 tablespoons sugar

1 teaspoon instant coffee granules (optional)

Filling

8 ounces semisweet chocolate, finely chopped

24 ounces cream cheese, softened

³/₄ cup sugar

3 eggs, at room temperature

2 teaspoons vanilla extract

2 teaspoons instant coffee granules

1 cup sour cream, at room temperature

To Serve

1 cup fresh raspberries

1 cup heavy whipping cream, whipped

Preheat the oven to 300 degrees.

For the crust, combine the cookie crumbs, butter, sugar and coffee granules in a bowl and mix well. Press over the bottom and up the side of a well-greased 9-inch springform pan. The crumbs should go up to the rim of the pan.

For the filling, melt the chocolate and set aside. Beat the cream cheese and sugar in a mixing bowl until light and fluffy. Beat in the eggs, vanilla and coffee granules. Stir in the chocolate and sour cream and blend until smooth.

Place the prepared springform pan on a baking sheet and pour the filling into the crust. Bake in the center of the oven for 1¹/₄ hours or until browned and puffed up in the center. Turn off the oven and let the cheesecake cool in the oven for 2 hours. Open the door periodically to let some of the heat escape to prevent the cheesecake from falling. Chill, tightly covered, in the refrigerator for 12 hours or until the center is completely set.

To serve, run a knife around the outside edge to loosen the crust. Remove the side of the pan. Cut the cheesecake into twelve slices. Place each slice on a dessert plate and garnish with raspberries and whipped cream.

Serves 12

Margarita Cheesecake

Crust

    4 ounces salted pretzels
      (to make 1 cup crumbs)
  1/3 cup sugar
  1/4 cup (1/2 stick) butter, melted

Filling

  24 ounces cream cheese, softened
    1 cup sour cream
  3/4 cup sugar
    2 tablespoons Grand Marnier or
      Triple Sec
    1 tablespoon tequila
    1 tablespoon grated lime zest
    4 eggs
      Lime slices

Preheat the oven to 375 degrees.

For the crust, place the pretzels in a food processor and pulse until fine crumbs form. Add the sugar and melted butter and process until blended.

Press the mixture evenly over the bottom and 1 inch up the side of a 9-inch springform pan. Place on a baking sheet. Bake for 5 to 7 minutes or until golden brown; cool.

For the filling, reduce the oven temperature to 325 degrees. Beat the cream cheese in a large mixing bowl for 1 minute or until light and fluffy. Beat in the sour cream, sugar, Grand Marnier, tequila and lime zest until smooth. Add the eggs one at a time, beating well after each addition.

Wrap the bottom and side of the springform pan with foil. Pour the filling into the cooled crust (it will come up higher than the crust). Place in a roasting pan; pour in enough hot water to come halfway up the side of the pan.

Bake in the center of the oven for 1 hour and 10 minutes or until the cheesecake is set and slightly firm to the touch. Remove to a wire rack and let cool completely. Chill, tightly covered, in the refrigerator for 4 hours or longer before serving. Garnish with lime slices.

Serve 12

This is a wonderful finale to a summer barbecue! Try it following Halibut with Citrus Pineapple Salsa (page 118).

Pumpkin Cheesecake

Crust

2 cups crushed gingersnaps
2 to 3 tablespoons butter, melted

Filling

16 ounces cream cheese, softened
3/4 cup sugar
4 eggs
1 1/2 cups (12 ounces) canned
    pumpkin
2 teaspoons pumpkin pie spice

Topping

1/2 cup chopped pecans
1/3 cup packed brown sugar
1 tablespoon maple syrup

Preheat the oven to 325 degrees.

For the crust, combine the gingersnaps and butter in a bowl and mix well. Press evenly over the bottom and up the side of a 9-inch springform pan.

For the filling, beat the cream cheese and sugar in a mixing bowl until light and fluffy. Add the eggs one at a time, beating well after each addition. Add the pumpkin and pumpkin pie spice, beating until smooth. Pour the filling into the crust and place on a baking sheet.

For the topping, combine the pecans, brown sugar and maple syrup in a bowl and mix well; set aside.

Bake for 40 minutes and sprinkle with the topping. Return to the oven and bake for 10 to 15 minutes longer or until the center is set but will still shake slightly. Cool completely at room temperature. Chill, covered, in the refrigerator before serving.

Serves 12

Washington Apple Cake

13/4 cups sugar
3 eggs
11/2 cups vegetable oil
1/4 cup orange juice
3 cups all-purpose flour
1 teaspoon baking soda
1/4 teaspoon salt
1 tablespoon ground cinnamon
1/2 teaspoon nutmeg
1 tablespoon vanilla extract
3 cups peeled finely
chopped apples
1 cup shredded coconut
1 cup chopped walnuts
Cream Cheese Icing

Preheat the oven to 325 degrees.

Combine the sugar, eggs, oil, orange juice, flour, baking soda, salt, cinnamon, nutmeg and vanilla in a large mixing bowl and mix well. Fold in the apples, coconut and walnuts.

Spoon the cake batter into a well-greased tube pan or bundt pan. Bake for 11/2 hours or until a wooden pick inserted into the center comes out clean. Let stand for 1 hour and turn onto a wire rack to cool completely. Frost with Cream Cheese Icing.

Serves 10 to 12

Cream Cheese Icing

6 ounces cream cheese, softened
1/4 cup (1/2 stick) butter, melted
2 cups confectioners' sugar
2 teaspoons vanilla extract
1/4 teaspoon lemon juice

Beat the cream cheese and butter in a mixing bowl until smooth. Add the confectioners' sugar, vanilla and lemon juice, beating until smooth. Spread over the cooled Washington Apple Cake.

Note: Apples are the largest crop grown in Washington State. Ten to twelve billion apples are hand-picked in Washington each year.

Molten Chocolate Cakes

1/2 cup (1 stick) butter
4 squares (4 ounces) bittersweet chocolate
2 eggs
2 egg yolks
1/4 cup sugar
2 teaspoons all-purpose flour
Ice cream or whipped cream

Preheat the oven to 450 degrees.

Place the butter and chocolate in the top of a double boiler set over simmering water. Heat until the chocolate is almost completely melted. Beat the eggs, egg yolks and sugar in a mixing bowl with an electric mixer until thick and fluffy.

Remove the chocolate mixture from the heat; beat until smooth. Add the egg mixture and flour, beating just until combined.

Butter and lightly flour four 4-ounce miniature bundt cake molds, custard cups or ramekins, tapping out any excess flour. Divide the batter evenly among the molds and place on a baking sheet. (At this point, you can refrigerate the cakes until ready to bake. Bring to room temperature before baking.)

Bake for 6 to 7 minutes or until the sides are set but the centers are still very soft. Remove from the oven and carefully invert each mold onto a plate. Let stand for about 10 seconds. (Unmold by lifting up one corner of the mold; the cake should fall onto the plate.) Serve immediately with ice cream or whipped cream.

Serves 4

Wine—Part III

Looking for something new and exciting? Knipprath Winery, a relative newcomer established in 1999, is noted for its Pinot Noir and Chocolate Port, both "local firsts." Or try Lone Canary's uniquely blended red wines, featuring "different regional styles." At Barrister Winery, started by two local attorneys, sample richly satisfying red wines and see why it is noted in the Wine Press Northwest as "one of the Northwest's emerging superstar wineries." Another boutique winery, Robert Karl, specializes in "luxury premium Bordeaux-style wine from Washington vineyards." Any of these wines are sure to make your next dinner party memorable.

Low-Fat Bread Pudding with Caramel Whiskey Sauce

1 (10-ounce) baguette, cut into 1-inch-thick slices
1/4 cup (1/2 stick) light butter, melted
1/2 cup raisins
1/4 cup Irish whiskey
1 3/4 cups low-fat milk
1 cup sugar
1 tablespoon vanilla extract
1 (12-ounce) can fat-free evaporated milk
2 eggs, lightly beaten
1 tablespoon sugar
1 teaspoon ground cinnamon
Caramel Whiskey Sauce

Preheat the oven to 350 degrees.

Arrange the baguette slices on a baking sheet and brush the tops with the butter. Bake for 10 minutes or until lightly toasted. Remove to a wire rack to cool. Cut into 1/2-inch cubes.

Combine the raisins and whiskey in a small bowl. Let stand, covered, for 10 minutes or until soft; do not drain.

Whisk the milk, 1 cup sugar, the vanilla, evaporated milk and eggs in a bowl until blended. Add the bread cubes and raisin mixture, stirring to coat. Let stand for 15 minutes.

Reheat the oven to 350 degrees. Spoon the mixture into a 9×13-inch baking dish coated with nonstick cooking spray. Combine 1 tablespoon sugar and 1 teaspoon cinnamon in a small bowl and mix well. Sprinkle the mixture over the bread pudding. Bake for 35 minutes or until set. Serve warm with Caramel-Whiskey Sauce.

Serves 10 to 12

Caramel Whiskey Sauce

1 1/2 cups sugar
2/3 cup water
1/4 cup (1/2 stick) light butter, softened
2 ounces 1/3-less-fat cream cheese, softened
1/4 cup Irish whiskey
1/4 cup 1% milk

Combine the sugar and water in a small heavy saucepan over medium-high heat. Cook until the sugar dissolves, stirring constantly. Cook for 15 minutes longer or until golden brown; do not stir. Remove from the heat. Add the butter and cream cheese, stirring constantly with a whisk until smooth. (Be careful, as the mixture will be hot and will bubble vigorously.) Cool slightly; stir in the whiskey and milk.

Pour the sauce over the warm bread pudding.

Pumpkin Cake Roll

Pumpkin Roll

   3 eggs
   1 cup sugar
   1 teaspoon lemon juice
   1 teaspoon baking soda
   1 teaspoon ground ginger
2/3 cup canned pumpkin
3/4 cup all-purpose flour
   2 teaspoons ground cinnamon
1/2 teaspoon nutmeg
1/2 teaspoon salt
     Chopped walnuts or flaked coconut (optional)

Cream Cheese Filling

   6 ounces cream cheese, softened
1/4 cup (1/2 stick) margarine, melted
   1 cup confectioners' sugar
   1 teaspoon vanilla extract

To Serve

     Confectioners' sugar

Preheat the oven to 375 degrees.

For the cake, beat the eggs at high speed with an electric mixer in a mixing bowl for 5 minutes. Add the sugar, lemon juice, baking soda, ginger, pumpkin, flour, cinnamon, nutmeg and salt and beat until smooth.

Spread the mixture in a 10×15-inch cake roll pan lined with baking parchment. Sprinkle with walnuts. Bake for 15 minutes.

Turn out onto a waxed paper-lined flat surface. Remove the baking parchment from the bottom and roll up the cake, jelly-roll fashion; let cool.

For the filling, beat the cream cheese and margarine in a mixing bowl until smooth. Add the confectioners' sugar and vanilla, beating until smooth.

Unroll the cooled cake and spread evenly with the filling. Reroll the cake and place seam side down on a serving platter.

To serve, dust generously with confectioners' sugar.

Serves 8 to 10

Bailey's Irish Cream Cake

Chocolate Ganache

1 cup heavy cream
16 ounces semisweet
chocolate chips

Devil's Food Cake

2 cups all-purpose flour
2 cups sugar
1/2 cup baking cocoa
1 tablespoon salt
1 tablespoon baking soda
1 egg, beaten
3/4 cup canola oil or vegetable oil
1 cup plus 2 tablespoons milk
1 cup plus 2 tablespoons hot
brewed coffee

Infusion

2/3 cup Bailey's Irish cream

For the ganache, bring the cream to a boil in a saucepan over medium-high heat. Remove from the heat and add the chocolate chips. Stir slowly until the chocolate is melted. Whisk the mixture briskly until smooth and shiny. Pour into a bowl and cool completely.

For the cake, preheat the oven to 350 degrees. Grease and flour two 9-inch cake pans. Combine the flour, sugar, baking cocoa, salt and baking soda in the bowl of an electric mixer and mix gently. Add the egg, canola oil, milk and coffee slowly, scraping the side and bottom of the bowl between each addition. Mix at medium speed until smooth. Pour the batter into the prepared pans. Bake for 25 to 30 minutes or until moist and firm to the touch. Remove to a wire rack and cool completely.

For the infusion, place one layer of the cake on a serving plate and prick several times with a skewer. Pour 1/3 cup of the Irish cream slowly over the top of the cake, letting it soak into the holes. Frost the cake layer with one-fourth of the ganache. Place the second layer on top. Prick the top with more holes and pour the remaining 1/3 cup Irish cream over the top. Add wooden picks to stabilize the cake if needed. Frost the entire cake with the remaining ganache. Wipe the serving plate around the cake clean before serving.

Note: This cake will keep several days in the refrigerator.

Tip: When cutting the cake, use a hot wet knife so the ganache stays together. Also, if you are short on time, replace the cake ingredients with a box of devil's food cake mix. Just use the directions on the package to prepare the cake, and then follow the remaining steps in this recipe.

Serves 8 to 10

Try this with our recipe for Grady's Irish Cream (page 37) to really wow your guests!

Lemon Huckleberry Pound Cake

1 cup (2 sticks) butter, softened
1³/4 cups sugar
3 eggs
3 cups all-purpose flour
1/2 teaspoon baking soda
1/2 teaspoon salt
1 cup buttermilk
3 tablespoons grated lemon zest
1/4 cup fresh lemon juice
1¹/2 cups fresh huckleberries
   or blueberries
   Lemon Cream Cheese Frosting

Preheat the oven to 325 degrees. Grease and flour a 10-inch bundt pan. Beat the butter and sugar in a large mixing bowl with an electric mixer until light and fluffy. Beat in the eggs one at a time until smooth. Combine the flour, baking soda and salt in a bowl and mix well. Add 1 cup to the butter mixture, alternating with 1/3 cup buttermilk and beating well after each addition. Repeat until all of the flour mixture and buttermilk have been used. Add the lemon zest and lemon juice and beat until blended. Pour half the batter into the prepared bundt pan. Scatter the huckleberries over the batter and cover with the remaining batter.

Bake for 1¹/4 hours or until a wooden pick inserted into the center comes out clean. Cool in the pan for 10 minutes and invert onto a serving platter. Cool completely and frost with Lemon Cream Cheese Frosting.

Serves 8 to 10

Lemon Cream Cheese Frosting

16 ounces cream cheese, softened
3/4 cup (1¹/2 sticks) butter, softened
4 cups confectioners' sugar
1 teaspoon grated lemon zest
1 teaspoon vanilla extract

Beat the cream cheese and butter in a large mixing bowl using an electric mixer until light and fluffy. Beat in the confectioners' sugar gradually. Beat in the lemon zest and vanilla. Chill, covered, in the refrigerator for 30 minutes or just until firm enough to spread.

Note: This makes more than enough frosting for the pound cake. The leftovers will keep in the refrigerator for up to 1 week.

Makes 4¹/2 cups

Chocolate and Kahlúa Ice Cream Pie

1 cup chocolate cookie crumbs
1/4 cup sugar
1/4 cup (1/2 stick) butter, softened
1/2 pint butter pecan ice
cream, softened
3 cups Kahlúa Chocolate Sauce
1 1/2 pints coffee ice cream, softened
1 cup heavy whipping cream

Combine the cookie crumbs, sugar and butter in a bowl and mix well. Press the mixture lightly over the bottom of a 9-inch pie plate. Freeze the crust for 1 hour. Spread the butter pecan ice cream over the crust in an even layer. Spread 3 tablespoons of the Kahlúa Chocolate Sauce over the butter pecan ice cream and return the pie to the freezer. Freeze until the ice cream is firm. Spread the coffee ice cream over the pie, mounding it slightly in the center. Return the pie to the freezer. When the ice cream is firm, wrap the pie tightly in plastic wrap. The pie will keep in the freezer for up to 1 week. To serve, remove the pie from the freezer and let soften for awhile in the refrigerator. Whip the cream and warm the remaining Kahlúa Chocolate Sauce. Cut the pie into slices and place on individual serving plates. Drizzle with sauce and garnish with a dollop of the whipped cream.

Serves 8

Kahlúa Chocolate Sauce

3/4 cup (1 1/2 sticks) unsalted butter
6 ounces semisweet
chocolate, chopped
3/4 cup plus 2 tablespoons sugar
3/4 cup lightly packed Dutch process
baking cocoa
1 1/2 teaspoons instant coffee granules
1/2 cup light corn syrup
3/4 cup heavy cream
1/2 cup Kahlúa
1 teaspoon vanilla extract

Melt the butter and chocolate in a saucepan over low heat, stirring until smooth. Whisk in the sugar until blended. Add the baking cocoa, coffee granules and corn syrup, whisking constantly. Whisk in the cream and Kahlúa slowly. Bring to a boil, stirring frequently. Reduce the heat and simmer for 5 minutes. Remove from the heat and stir in the vanilla. Pour the sauce into a heatproof container with a lid. Cool completely at room temperature. Chill, covered, in the refrigerator for 24 hours to let the flavors blend. Reheat in the microwave or in a saucepan over low heat. Refrigerate the remaining sauce in a tightly sealed jar for several months.

Serves 10

Frozen Mint Truffle Pie

Crust

1¼ cups chocolate cookie crumbs

2 tablespoons butter, melted

Filling

1 cup (2 sticks) butter, softened

2 cups confectioners' sugar

4 ounces unsweetened chocolate, melted and cooled

4 eggs

¾ teaspoon peppermint flavoring

1 teaspoon vanilla extract

Chocolate cookie crumbs

Fresh mint leaves

For the crust, combine the cookie crumbs and butter in a bowl and mix well. Press the mixture onto the bottom and up the side of a 9-inch pie plate.

For the filling, beat the butter and confectioners' sugar in a mixing bowl with an electric mixer until light and fluffy. Add the chocolate and beat until smooth. Beat in the eggs one at a time. Beat in the peppermint flavoring and vanilla. Pour the filling into the crust and smooth the surface. Sprinkle a few cookie crumbs in the center of the pie. Freeze for 2½ to 3 hours or until firm. Let stand at room temperature for 10 minutes to soften before slicing. Garnish with fresh mint leaves.

Tip: Use a premade chocolate crumb piecrust if you are short on time. This can also be made into individual servings by pressing the crust mixture into cupcake wrappers placed in muffin cups and dividing the filling evenly.

Serves 8

If you are concerned about using raw eggs, use eggs pasteurized in their shells, which are sold at some specialty food stores, or use an equivalent amount of pasteurized egg substitute.

Strawberry Cheesecake Ice Cream Roll

1/2 gallon ice cream
(square container)
18 graham cracker squares, crushed
1 cup sliced strawberries
3 cups chopped cheesecake,
crust removed
1/3 cup honey
Honey, strawberries or
sprigs of fresh mint

Line a 9×13-inch baking sheet with baking parchment. Remove the paper packaging from the block of ice cream. Cut the ice cream into 1/2-inch slices. Lay four slices in a row on the lined baking sheet. Blend the seams together with a spatula to create one full sheet of ice cream. Refreeze the ice cream for 20 minutes or until firm.

Sprinkle the ice cream with the graham cracker crumbs, 1 cup strawberries and the cheesecake and drizzle with 1/3 cup honey.

Starting on a lengthwise edge of the ice cream, peel away the baking parchment and begin rolling to create a log. Roll to enclose the filling and bring the two lengthwise sides together. Blend the seams together with a spatula to create a seamless look. Wrap the log in baking parchment and freeze until ready to serve.

To serve, cut into slices and garnish with honey, strawberries or fresh mint sprigs.

Serves 12

Try making an Oreo Honey Ice Cream Roll. Prepare the roll exactly as described above, substituting 15 to 20 crushed Oreos and 3/4 cup chopped pecans for the graham crackers, strawberries and cheesecake. Garnish as above, adding chocolate-covered espresso beans as an extra chocolatey touch.

Soft Molasses Cookies

1¹/₂ cups shortening
2 cups granulated sugar
¹/₂ cup light molasses
2 eggs
4 cups all-purpose flour
¹/₂ teaspoon salt
4 teaspoons baking soda
2 teaspoons ground cinnamon
2 teaspoons ground cloves
2 teaspoons ground ginger
Granulated sugar for coating
Confectioners' sugar (optional)

Preheat the oven to 375 degrees.

Cream the shortening and 2 cups granulated sugar in a mixing bowl until light and fluffy. Beat in the molasses and eggs. Add the flour, salt, baking soda, cinnamon, cloves and ginger and mix well. Shape into balls. Roll the balls in granulated sugar to coat and place on a cookie sheet. Bake small balls for 7 to 8 minutes or until crisp around the edge and large balls for 8 to 10 minutes or until soft. Sift confectioners' sugar over the cookies. Store in an airtight container.

Makes 4 dozen small or 2¹/₂ dozen large cookies

Crunchy Chocolate Chip Cookies

$^{1}/_{2}$ cup (1 stick) butter, softened
$^{1}/_{2}$ cup granulated sugar
$^{1}/_{2}$ cup packed brown sugar
 1 egg
 1 teaspoon milk
 1 teaspoon vanilla extract
$1^{3}/_{4}$ cups all-purpose flour
$1^{1}/_{2}$ teaspoons baking soda
$^{1}/_{2}$ teaspoon salt
 6 tablespoons vegetable oil
$^{1}/_{2}$ cup cornflakes
$^{1}/_{2}$ cup quick-cooking oats
 6 to 8 ounces chocolate chips

Preheat the oven to 350 degrees.

Beat the butter, granulated sugar and brown sugar in a mixing bowl until light and fluffy. Add the egg, milk and vanilla, beating until smooth.

Sift the flour, baking soda and salt into a bowl.

Add to the butter mixture alternately with the oil, mixing well after each addition.

Stir in the cornflakes, oats and chocolate chips. Drop by teaspoonfuls onto a cookie sheet. Bake for 9 to 10 minutes. Remove to a wire rack to cool.

Makes $4^{1}/_{2}$ dozen small cookies

The cornflakes give these cookies an intriguing crunch that makes them irresistible.

Angelic Almond Bars

First Layer

  2 cups all-purpose flour
1/4 cup water
  1 cup (2 sticks) butter or
     margarine, cut into small pieces

Second Layer

12 ounces cream cheese, softened
3/4 cup sugar
1½ teaspoons almond extract
  3 eggs

Frosting

2¼ cups confectioners' sugar
2¼ tablespoons milk
1/3 cup margarine, softened
1½ teaspoons almond extract
    Sliced toasted almonds

Preheat the oven to 350 degrees.

For the first layer, combine the flour and water in a bowl, stirring until crumbly. Cut in the butter until the mixture resembles coarse crumbs. Press the mixture over the bottom of a 9×13-inch baking pan. Bake for 10 minutes.

For the second layer, beat the cream cheese and sugar in a mixing bowl with an electric mixer for 3 minutes or until light and fluffy. Add the almond extract and the eggs one at a time, beating until smooth. Spread the mixture over the bottom layer. Bake for 15 to 20 minutes. Remove to a wire rack to cool.

For the frosting, combine the confectioners' sugar, milk, margarine and almond extract in a mixing bowl and beat at low speed until combined. Beat at high speed until lightly whipped. Spread the frosting over the cooled layers. Top with sliced toasted almonds. To serve, cut into bars.

Serves 12

Apricot Logs

1 cup dried apricots
1/4 cup granulated sugar
8 ounces apricot preserves
2 tablespoons brandy
1 (14-ounce) package frozen puff pastry sheets, thawed
1/4 cup bread crumbs
1 egg white
1 tablespoon water
1/2 cup clear sugar crystals or raw sugar

Preheat the oven to 375 degrees.

Place the apricots in the food processor with the granulated sugar. Pulse until the apricots are coarsely ground. Add the apricot preserves and brandy and pulse to combine. Place the mixture in a medium bowl.

Roll out one sheet of puff pastry on a pastry cloth dusted lightly with flour. Roll the dough into a 14×16-inch rectangle. Repeat with the remaining sheet of puff pastry. The pastry should be cool but not cold.

Cut each rectangle into three long strips about 4¹/3×16 inches each. Add the bread crumbs to the apricot mixture and mix well. Spoon the mixture into a pastry bag with a large 1/2-inch-wide tip. Squeeze an even line of filling (about 1/2 inch wide) down the center of each pastry strip.

Lightly beat the egg white and water in a small bowl until blended. Brush the long edges of each pastry sheet with some of the egg white mixture. Fold the edges over the apricot filling to form a long thick roll. Seal the rolls carefully, brushing with additional egg white mixture. Sprinkle with the sugar crystals. Cut the pastry rolls at 2-inch intervals with a pizza wheel to make small logs.

Place the logs on baking parchment-lined baking sheets. Bake for 20 to 25 minutes or until the tops are lightly browned and the pastry is puffed. Let cool on the pans for 1 minute; remove to a wire rack to cool completely.

Note: The logs freeze well and can be reheated to maintain crispness. Good warm or at room temperature.

Makes 50 (2-inch) logs

Scrumptious Peanut Butter Brownies

3 eggs
2 cups sugar
1 cup (2 sticks) butter or
  margarine, melted
2 teaspoons vanilla extract
1 1/4 cups all-purpose flour
3/4 cup baking cocoa
1/2 teaspoon baking powder
1/4 teaspoon salt
1 1/2 cups semisweet chocolate chips
8 ounces cream cheese, softened
3/4 cup creamy peanut butter
1/4 cup sugar
1 egg
2 tablespoons milk

Preheat the oven to 350 degrees.

Cream the eggs, 2 cups sugar, the butter and vanilla in a large mixing bowl with an electric mixer until light and fluffy. Combine the flour, baking cocoa, baking powder and salt in a bowl and mix well. Add to the egg mixture and mix well. Stir in the chocolate chips. Set aside 1 cup of batter for the topping. Spread the remaining batter in a greased 9×13-inch baking pan.

Beat the cream cheese, peanut butter and 1/4 cup sugar in a bowl until smooth. Add the egg and milk, beating at low speed just until combined. Carefully spread over the brownie batter. Drop the reserved brownie batter by tablespoonfuls over the filling. Cut through the batter with a knife to swirl. Bake for 35 to 40 minutes or until a wooden pick inserted into the center comes out clean. Remove to a wire rack and let cool. Chill, covered, in the refrigerator before serving.

Makes 3 dozen brownies

Almond Popcorn Clusters

1 cup sugar
1/4 cup water
1 tablespoon almond extract
1/3 cup light corn syrup
1/2 cup (1 stick) butter
1 cup popcorn kernels, popped
2 ounces sliced almonds

Combine the sugar, water, almond extract and corn syrup in a medium saucepan. Boil over medium-high heat until the sugar dissolves, stirring constantly. Add the butter, stirring to blend. Boil until the mixture reaches 225 degrees (soft-ball stage) on a candy thermometer. Remove from the heat. Place the popcorn in a large heatproof bowl. Pour the hot syrup slowly over the popcorn. Add the almonds and mix well. Let cool. Break into clusters and store in a tightly covered container.

Makes about 20 clusters

White Velvet Cut-Outs

Cookies

- 2 cups (4 sticks) butter or margarine, softened
- 8 ounces cream cheese, softened
- 2 cups sugar
- 2 egg yolks
- 1 teaspoon vanilla extract
- 4¹/2 cups all-purpose flour

Frosting

- 3¹/2 cups confectioners' sugar
- 3 tablespoons butter or margarine, softened
- 1 teaspoon vanilla extract
- 3 to 4 tablespoons evaporated milk
  Food coloring

Preheat the oven to 350 degrees.

For the cookies, cream the butter and cream cheese in a mixing bowl until light and fluffy. Add the sugar, egg yolks and vanilla, beating until smooth. Add the flour gradually, mixing well after each addition. Chill, covered, in the refrigerator for 2 hours or until firm.

Roll out the dough to ¹/4-inch thickness on a smooth lightly floured surface. Cut into shapes with cookie cutters and place on a greased cookie sheet. Bake for 10 to 12 minutes. Remove to a wire rack to cool.

For the frosting, combine 1¹/2 cups of the confectioners' sugar, the butter, vanilla and 3 tablespoons evaporated milk in a mixing bowl. Beat until smooth. Add the remaining 2 cups confectioners' sugar gradually. Beat for 3 minutes or until light and fluffy. Add enough of the remaining 1 tablespoon evaporated milk and several drops of food coloring to reach the desired color and consistency. Frost the cooled cookies.

Makes 7 dozen cookies

These cut-out cookies have crisp edges and a tangy taste like a soft shortbread cookie.

STILL GOLD'N Committee

Chairperson   Kristine Bedford-Lyons
Chairpersons Elect   Stephanie Combs
Diane Jeckle
Debra Sidor-Tanner

Editors & Non-Recipe Text   Kristine Bedford-Lyons
Amy Garvin
Michelle Grady
Shannon Grady

Cookbook Committee   Meghan Anderson
Holly Austin
Kristine Bedford-Lyons
Lexi Burg
Libby Cousins
Amy Garvin
Michelle Grady
Diane Jeckle
Shelby Johnson
Debbie Liberg
Kristin Markham
Catherine O'Connell
Gaye Shumaker
Abbi Spilker
Kerrianne Thronson
Krissy Wilcox
Kathleen Wynia

Chapter Chairs

Appetizers, Beverages & Cocktails   Holly Austin
Catherine O'Connell

Breads & Brunch   Michelle Grady

Soups, Salads & Sides   Libby Cousins
Amy Garvin
Diane Jeckle

Meat & Poultry   Kerrianne Thronson

Pasta & Seafood   Debbie Liberg

Desserts   Krissy Wilcox

Underwriting   Paula Johnson
Catherine O'Connell

Sustaining Advisor   Paula Johnson

On behalf of the cookbook committee, our deepest thanks to Spokane Junior League members and sustainers, their families, and friends. Without your efforts and support, this book would not have been possible.

The Junior League of Spokane thanks its members, both active and sustaining, and their families and friends who contributed to this book. We sincerely hope that no one has been missed.

Stephanie Aden
Eleanor Anderson
Jennie Anderson
Laura Anderson
Marianne Anderson*
Meghan & Scott Anderson
Robin & David Anderson
Beverly Altringer
Sandy Altringer
Holly Austin
Betty Backstrom
Jodie Bailey
Jane Baldwin
Dorothy Benson
Lorrie Bernardi
Sharon Bernardi
Seanna & Kell Bodholt
LeAnne Bonham & Family
Sharon Bradley
Liz Bratcher
Edith Bressler
Donna Brewster
Ann Briggs
Richard Brooke
Greg Brown
Sandi Buche
Lexi & Gary Burg
Linda Burgin
Joe Busch

MaryAnn Busch
Ginger Carter
Mike Centrone
Carolyn Chambers
Kelly Chapin
Faris Charbonneau
Nena Chavez
Marshall Chesrown
Ginger & Ed Clark
Julie & Darryle Clark
Stephanie & John Combs
Katie Cotter
Brooke & Trent Cousins
Libby & Allen Cousins
Barbara Cozza
Julie Crance
Vicki Craigen
Alanna & Jim Crouch*
Dr. Christi Culp
Marti & Mark D'Agostino
Candace Dahlstrom-Mumm
Janice D'Aloia
Ethel Davis
Louann & Chester Davis
Janice Deardorff
Fred DeFord
Angela & John Delay
Kim Delich
Everett Doolittle

Melissa Dulin
Sharon Dunn
Emily Estess
Marietta & Mike F. Estess
Michael P. Estess
Joanne Evans
Mary Evans
Jody Fergin
Doug Ferrante
Joanne Ferris
Sharon Fioritto
Laura Fiske
Susan Flatow
Stacy & Jeff Folkins
Andrea Frank
Gaylan Frederic
Kathy Friedlander
Anna & Dan Fritts
Jan Gabrio
Amy & Steve Garvin
Cindy & Matt Garvin
Jack Garvin
Sarah Garvin
Stephne & Woody Garvin
Thorne Garvin
Melissa George
Jack Geraghty
Sheila Geraghty
Carolee Giersdorf

Vicki Gifford
Bill Gilchrist
Candi Morton Gilchrist
KayDee Gilkey
Mackenzie Grady
Madison Grady
MaDonna Grady
Michelle & Shannon Grady
Ryan Grady
Kristin Griffith
Cole Grogan
Ryan Grogan
Tricia & Greg Grogan
Marianne Guenther
Amy Gustaveson & Family
Greg Hagen
JoAnn Hagen
Lisa Hagen
Molly Hagen
Tony Hagen
Patty Hallinan
Donna Halvorson
Heidi & Mike Harrington
Nancy Hawley
Brett Heberer
Kay Heberer
Luke Heberer
Melanie & Matt Heberer
Kathy Heimbigner

Rod Heimbigner
Marilyn Henderson
Jacky Herrington
Kitty Hess
Marcy Holland
Elaine Holliday
Cathryn Hurley*
Diane & Bill Jeckle
Jean & Milan Jeckle
Ann Johnson
Chrissy Johnson
Janece Johnson
Paula & Randy Johnson
Shelby & Scott Johnson
Carole Jones*
Colleen & Bruce Kelly
Cindy Kennedy
Stu Kinzebach
Diane Klein*
Shannon Knight
Dolores & Jerry Kofmehl
Jannel & Pat Kofmehl
Leesa & Wayne Kofmehl
Shelly Kuney
Andre LaSalle
Gretchen LaSalle
Kathy LaSalle
Marion LaSalle
Donna Lee

Terry Lewis
Tim Lewis
Connie Liberg
Debbie & Brian Liberg
Helen Liberg
Hunter Liberg
Jonathan Liberg
Madeline Liberg
Ray Liberg
Ryan Liberg
Tambra Liberg
Sheri Longhenry
Gloria M. Lopez
John Love
Kristina Love
Jane Lyons
Joseph Lyons
Kevin Lyons
Kristine & John Lyons
Niall Lyons
Nicholas Lyons
Mike Macaulay
Melissa Magnuson
Susie Maher
Leslie Mallett
Lynn Mandyke
Cari Manry
Carl Manry
Charles "Skip" Manry
Christopher Manry
Kristin Markham
Beth Marshall

Cheryl Martin
Kris & Scott Mason
Bob McDaniel
Andrea McFarland
Julia McGann
Julie Melby
Allison & Andrew Miller
Catherine Miller
Erin Miller
Matt Miller
Anne Minion
Corabelle Minion
Cathy & Dave Moczulski
Mary Moloney
Judy & Stan Moore
Carol Mueller
Julie Munson
Carol Neupert*
Sarah Neupert
Kelley & Buzz Nielsen
John Nielsen
Lisa Nielsen
Maureen O'Brien*
Catherine O'Connell
Topper O'Connell
Barbie Olsen
Patty Osterman
Glenda & Scott Pearson
Nathan Pearson
Bridget Piper
Mary Potter
Colleen Quine

Hailey Rademacher
Meredith Remme
Kathy Reugh
Loni Reynolds
Kati Rhoades
Sherri Ritter
Janelle Rogers
BJ Ross
Holly & Bruce Ross
Tia Rupe
Doug Russell
Nancy Russell
The Russell Clan
Paul St. Hiliare
Tracey & Jay St. Onge
Tina Santorsola
Marley Scheckler
Anita Scheer
Bill Scheer
Emily Scheer
Therese Schmarr
Jamie Severson
Cindy & Chris Sexton
Betty Shanks
Tom Shanks
Jinger & Tyler Shoemaker
Christian Shook
Gaye Shumaker
Debra Sidor-Tanner
Diane Sidor
Patricia Sidor
Vicki Simmons

Lois Solheim
Abbi & John Spilker
Becky Spilker
Jon Spilker
Katharine Spilker
Krista & Molly Spilker
Olivia Spilker
Katie & Brad Stark
Tammy Starkey
Marilyn Stocker
Corena Stretch
Linda Stokke
Mary Jane Sullivan
Paige & Kevin Swaim
Angela Swartout
Gina Symmes
Sue Thomas
Amy Thompson
Janis Thompson
Lynn & Bob Thomson
Kerrianne Thronson
Drew Timms
Barbara Tompkins
Benjamin Toole
Jeannette & Jeff Toole
Nicholas Toole
Tom Trask
Amy Tresko
Rick Utter
Mary Beth Van Winkle
Jill & Eric Wakeling
Kristine Walker

Robin Waller
Staci Ward
Rob Warhime
Carol Wendle*
Katie Wilcox
Krissy & John Wilcox
Sydney Wilcox
Andrea Wilde
Bobbi Wilson
Roger Wilson
Tammy Wilson
Glenda & Joe Winter
Molly Wright
Norma Jean Wold
Kathleen Wynia
Katie Wynia
Nancy & Dan Wynia
Terry Zalevitz
Alison Zecha

*Denotes contributors who donated to the *Still Gold'n* Cookbook fund

Chapter Sponsors

www.spokesmanreview.com

www.sterlingsavingsbank.com

www.greatharvest.com

Page Sponsors

www.watrust.com

www.thedavenporthotel.com

www.ezloader.com

www.blackrockdevelopment.com

www.farm-credit.com

www.aestheticimage.net

Supporters

www.combsortho.com

www.dci-engineers.com

INDEX

About Spokane

The Junior League of Spokane
1315 North Napa Street • Spokane, Washington 99202
509-328-2801 • Fax: 509-328-1827

Please send me _____ copies of *Still Gold'n* at $24.95 per book $ _____

Please send me _____ copies of *Gold'n Delicious Cookbook* at $22.95 per book $ _____

Purchase both books at $39.95 per set $ _____

Add postage and handling at $5.00 per book $ _____

Total $ _____

Name _____ Telephone _____

Address _____

City _____ State _____ Zip _____

Method of Payment: [   ] MasterCard   [   ] VISA   [   ] Check payable to the Junior League of Spokane

Account Number _____ Expiration Date _____

Signature _____

Photocopies will be accepted.